Austin Healey

100-6 & 3000

CW00956231

Also from Veloce Publishing:

First published in September 2007 by Veloce Publishing Limited, 33 Trinity Street, Dorchester DT1 1TT, England. Fax 01305 268864/e-mail info@veloce.co.uk/web www.veloce.co.uk or www.velocebooks.com.
ISBN: 978-1-845841-28-1/UPC: 6-36847-04128-1
Readers with ideas for automotive books, or books on other transport or related hobby subjects, are invited to write to the editorial director of Veloce Publishing at the above address.
British Library Cataloguing in Publication Data - A catalogue record for this book is available from the British Library. Typesetting, design and page make-up all by Veloce Publishing Ltd on Apple Mac.
Printed in India by Replika Press.

Austin Healey

100-6 & 3000

RALLY GIANTS

Graham Robson

Contents

Foreword

What is a rally? Today's events, for sure, are completely different from those of a hundred or even fifty years ago. What was once a test of reliability is now a test of speed and strength. What was once a long-distance trial is now a series of short-distance races.

In the beginning, rallying was all about using standard cars in long-distance road events, but by the 1950s the events were toughening up. Routes became rougher, target speeds were raised, point-to-point speed tests on special stages were introduced, and high-performance machines were needed to ensure victory.

Starting in the late 1950s, too, teams began developing extra-special versions of standard cars, these were built in small numbers, and were meant only to go rallying or motor racing. These 'homologation specials' now dominate the sport. The first of these, no question, was the Austin Healey 3000, which is profiled here, and the latest is any one of the ten-off World Rally Cars which we see on our TV screens, or on the special stages of the world. Although rally regulations changed persistently over the years, the two most important events were four-wheel drive being authorised from 1980, and the 'World Rally Car' formula (which required only 20 identical cars to be produced to gain homologation) being adopted in 1997. At all times,

however, successful rally cars have needed to blend high performance with strength and reliability. Unlike Grand Prix cars, they have needed to be built so that major repairs could be carried out at the side of the road, in the dark, sometimes in freezing cold, and sometimes in blazing temperatures.

Over the years, some cars became dominant, only to be eclipsed when new and more advanced rivals appeared. New cars appeared almost every year, but dramatically better machines appeared less often. From time to time rally enthusiasts would be astonished by a new model, and it was on occasions like that when a new rallying landmark was set.

So, which were the most important new cars to appear in the last half century? What is it that made them special at the time? In some cases it was perfectly obvious – Lancia's Stratos was the first-ever purpose-built rally car, the Audi Quattro was the first rally-winning four-wheel drive car, and the Toyota Celica GT4 was the first rally-winning four-wheel drive Group A car to come from Japan.

But what about the Big Healey? Ford's original Escort? Or the Fiat 131 Abarth? Or the Lancia Delta Integrale? Or, of course, the Subaru Impreza? All of them had something unique to offer at the time, in comparison with their competitors. Because they offered something different, and raised rallying's standards even further, they were true Rally Giants.

To a rallying petrol-head like me, it would have been easy to choose twenty, thirty or even more rally cars that have made a difference to the sport. However, I have had to be brutal and cull my list to the very minimum. Listed here, in chronological order, are the 'Giant' cars I have picked out, to tell the ongoing story of world-class rallying in the last fifty years:

Car	Period used as a works car
Austin Healey 3000	1959-1965
Saab 96 and V4	1960-1976
Mini Cooper/Cooper S	1962-1970
Ford Escort MkI	1968-1975
Lancia Stratos	1974-1981
Ford Escort MkII	1975-1981
Fiat 131 Abarth	1976-1981
Audi Quattro and S1	1981-1986
Peugeot 205 T16	1984-1986
Lancia Delta 4x4/Integrale	1987-1993
Toyota Celica GT4	1988-1995
Ford Escort RS Cosworth/WRC	1993-1998
Mitsubishi Lancer Evo	1995-2001
Subaru Impreza Turbo/WRC	1993-2006
Peugeot 206WRC	1999-2003
Ford Focus WRC	1999-2005

There is so much to know, to tell, and to enjoy about each of these cars that I plan to devote a compact book to each one. And to make sure that one can be compared with another, I intend to keep the same format for each volume.

Graham Robson

Introduction

It was BMC's much-respected competitions manager of the period, Marcus Chambers, who once commented about the Austin Healey that "we had long felt that we needed a car with long hairy legs to stride over the mountains and great lungs with which to rush up the hills: this seemed to be it."

And so it was. The 'Big Healey', as it was always affectionately known by the team, its drivers, and by millions of motoring enthusiasts, was the rally car which quite transformed the British Motor Corporation's rallying fortunes. By developing a solid, fast but conventional sports car into an amazingly charismatic, versatile and phenomenally rapid rally car, the dedicated works team at Abingdon, south of Oxford, produced the first true Rally Giant of all time.

It was the right car, at the right time, developed by the best people, and campaigned by some of the world's fastest and bravest rally drivers. Over time – and here was a car that was in regular works service for almost a decade – everyone connected with the Big Healey contributed. It was not only a car which saved BMC's stumbling rallying efforts from ridicule, but it also set standards that every other team needed to match.

The Big Healey – in particular the Austin Healey 3000 – became the world's first 'homologation special', and it therefore started a trend. It was the very first car in a long and distinguished line of competition cars which was especially developed, or evolved, to take every advantage of whatever regulations, and whatever categories, that motor sport had to offer at the time.

Well before any of their rivals, Marcus Chambers, Geoff Healey, and their enthusiastic colleagues realised that if their corporation did not already have an ideal car with which to go rallying, then they and their development engineers would have to devise one. If this meant going through the rule book with a fine-tooth comb, using up every allowance which was mentioned, and leaning hard on the literal meaning of some of them, so be it. BMC was not the only team to do this – let's just say that it was the first, and the standard-setter.

The way that the Big Healey was developed was a credit to any motor sport operation. Every detail in the specification – engine and tuning potential, transmission possibilities, chassis strengthening, the lightening of the body shell, reducing the vulnerability to underbody damage, and the ease of fettling the car at the side of the road – was considered. Right from the start, the Competitions Department knew what had to be done and, happily, management backed it almost all the way. Even so, when the Healey rally programme was seriously initiated in 1958, as a rally car it wasn't yet fast enough, not reliable enough, and not suited to every event the team chose to tackle.

Fortunately Abingdon was given time to make all the changes. In the next few years, improvements were brought forward in a steady stream for by observation, patient development, and sheer persistence, the deficiencies were gradually squeezed out of the same basic model. The definitive Big Healey which won Spa-Sofia-Liège in 1964 was a much faster, more reliable and altogether more formidable machine than that which had been used only six years earlier.

This, though, was never meant to be a rally car for 'everyman'. Unlike the Minis which were its stable mates in the 1960s, and the Ford Escorts which followed on, the works Healey was never meant to be the sort of rally car which could be replicated by the score, or especially by the hundred. Although most special competition parts were made available to the well-to-do private owner (they had to be, to meet the regulations), much of Abingdon's preparation expertise was never shared, and it was always clear to the average rally driver that these were cars which could not be used, year in and year out, because they would become battered into submission by awful roads, and cost a fortune to replace.

Accordingly, for years the nearest thing to a works Big Healey was one of the rare cars which was sold off from Abingdon when it was of no further use to the team. Since quite a few cars were literally written off, or unceremoniously scrapped, this meant that the supply was extremely limited.

Even so, there was always a queue for such rare beasts, because a Big Healey had something which an ex-works Triumph TR, or an ex-works Rapier, never had – and that was charisma. To stand alongside a Big Healey fresh out of an Alpine Rally speed test, or an RAC Rally special stage, when the car was hot and sticky, was like standing next to the horse that has just won the Grand National. Not only had it just been there, and done that – but it had usually done it in great style, and everyone loved it for that.

How to sum up this amazing rally car? It set new standards. Before the Big Healey, there were cars which could go rallying, and might occasionally win. After the Healey, though, a rally car had to be better, more special, and more dedicated to success. Not many were.

The car and the team

Inspiration

It's worth remembering that, in the beginning, neither Donald Healey, his design team nor anyone at the newly formed BMC Competitions Department at Abingdon ever thought that Austin Healeys might make successful rally cars: it was never intended. Originally, it was thought they might become useful racing machines, but as for rallying in the 1950s – that was not considered exciting enough or demanding enough at the time. How wrong they were! As every Austin Healey enthusiast knows, the six-cylinder engined cars – 100-Six and 3000 – went on to build memorable reputations in the sport as the most charismatic, rugged, and visually appealing rally cars of the period.

For almost ten years, in fact, the works Austin Healeys were the most famous – and glamorous – cars in international rallying. This sport changed considerably in the 1950s, with high performance and sheer strength becoming more and more essential; rapidly it demanded the evolution of fast and durable cars. Austin Healey successes at this level helped consolidate a remarkable image for the marque.

Even so, their basic layout was by no means ideal for the ever-more-demanding rally routes of the period. It was only the gritty determination and boundless experience of the BMC Competitions Department at Abingdon which helped turn these cars into rally winners. As I became more involved in the sport at this time, it was fascinating to see the way that the cars improved. By the early 1960s they had become proficient in every way – in performance, in reliability, and especially in versatility. They were not merely good in their category, but were contenders for outright victory wherever they appeared.

Looking back over half-a-century, it's easy to suggest that BMC (and Abingdon) wasted several valuable years before it began to develop the Austin Healey into a formidable works rally car, for even as a four-cylinder-engined car (the 100/4 and 100S) it could have been made competitive. Particularly with the 100S (and homologation could certainly have been

For special record attempts, Healey developed long-nose versions of the Austin Healey 100 for use on the Bonneville Salt Flats. Much of what was learned was later used in the works rally cars, too.

Early Austin Healeys were raced, but not rallied – this is one of the 'special test cars' competing at Le Mans in 1953.

'massaged' through the system in those more naïve days), it could have been turned into one of the toughest and fastest sports cars in the business.

There does not seem to have been any malicious reason, or incompetence, behind this; it was more a matter of benign neglect. The fact is that for the first few years of its career, nobody at Abingdon troubled to do any serious development of the Austin Healey because there seemed to be other priorities, and much more exciting things to concentrate on.

It was certainly not because the cars were basically unsuitable (in the 1960s, BMC soon proved otherwise!), but because the Healey family itself never really gave it a thought at first, and because BMC's newly-formed works Competitions Department concentrated on the use of other, more mundane, BMC models between 1955 and 1957.

Strange, though, isn't it? Even by 1955 it was clear that sports cars had a great future in international rallying. Triumph, from a standing start, had produced a successful works team of TR2s, and in spite of its cars' unpromising specification, Rootes had even wrung some success out of the heavy and under-powered Alpines and Rapiers. But, for the time being, the Healey family was not interested. In its first decade of life, the Healey company had built several fine and reliable endurance race cars – notably the Silverstone and Nash-Healey types – and was intent on doing even better with the lightweight 100S.

In any case, it wasn't long after the original 100/4 had gone on sale before British and European clubmen made their own assessment of standard types of Healey, and came to their own conclusions. By the time the rival TR2 and 100/4 cars were well-established, the received wisdom was that the Austin Healey handled well but was too low-slung for use in rallies (where the surfaces were often loose and sometimes rough – which might cause damage to the underside of the cars), while the Triumph TR2 didn't handle at all well, but was not as low, and seemed to be rugged enough for rallying work: in addition, it was significantly cheaper. The Big Healey, in other words, was soon seen as a useful machine for club racing, while the TR2 was soon preferred as a rally car.

Between 1954 and 1957, therefore, the works Triumphs had much of their own way in the hurly-burly of International rallying. Although these cars were never aggressively developed (the works TR2s and TR3s never used engines which were more powerful than standard, and there seemed to be no attempt to lighten them, or to make them special, for instance), and there never appeared to be a settled team of works drivers, they were usually reliable, and went on to pick up a series of impressive class and category wins in the Tulip, Alpine and Liège-Rome-Liège rallies.

It wasn't until BMC's works Competitions Department was freed from the dead weight of the sales department's marketing demands (was it ever likely that an Austin A50 or A90 could be made competitive enough to win anything? Maybe not, but the sales staff wanted to see the cars out on events), and was allowed to pick the best cars for the job, that it even began to look like a professional organisation. For the experienced Marcus Chambers this must have been a frustrating time, as his organisation spent its first three years fruitlessly grappling with cars like the Austin A90 Westminster, the Riley Pathfinder, the MG Magnette, and the nimble but under-powered MG MGA 1500.

A look through the records shows that in those formative years, a works Austin Healey was only entered on one occasion – when Peter Reece and Dennis Scott tackled the 1955 Liège-Rome-Liège Marathon in a 100S. This, in fact, was not an Abingdon car, but was one of the works 100S competition cars, which had been prepared and run from Warwick in long-distance races.

Like so many of BMC's rally entries of the period, the Liège entry was of the nature of a 'suck-it-and-see' experiment. Marcus Chambers wanted to see how a 100S would perform in an event where endurance and reliability had to be mixed with high performance. As he later wrote in his splendid book *Seven Year Twitch*: "The BMC entry was of a purely exploratory nature, the object being for two saloon cars to finish and demonstrate their reliability, with an Austin Healey 100S, making the best use of its superior performance – to finish as high as it could."

Would the 100S be competitive against the four-cam Porsche Carreras or the Mercedes-Benz 300SL sports cars which were dominating such events? We may never know how good this car should have been on the famous marathon, for it did not even survive the first night of this four-day non-stop slog from Belgium to Italy and back. It was crashed, in Germany, in thick fog, at a very early stage, and had to retire.

Marcus Chambers's comments in *Seven Year Twitch* spell out the farrago: "Dennis Scott had crashed the Healey at a corner on the way out of [Idar Oberstein]; he apparently went straight on, instead of turning to the right, and landed in a wood. Dennis and Peter abandoned the car to seek help, and on returning found that both the clocks and the spare wheel had been stolen. They returned rather sheepishly to Spa the next day."

After that disappointing experience, Marcus then abandoned ideas of using Austin Healeys for the next couple of years, though his team lacked cars with enough performance to tackle the European opposition on equal terms.

The Big Healey's importance in rallying

In the next few years, the Healey became important, not only to BMC, and its works efforts, but to the whole of European rallying. For the very first time, a resourceful team showed that if the commitment and expertise was made available, then there was enough scope in the latest homologation regulations to allow rather run-of-the-mill production cars to be turned into formidable special rally cars. Specialist knowledge and real determination were needed – and BMC had plenty of that.

As far as BMC was concerned, in the mid- and late-1950s, the six-cylinder Healey was almost the only production car in its sprawling range which showed any promise of becoming an outright rally winner, for, in general, BMC saloons were uninspiring and the MG sports cars were still under-powered. Other models might be cute, and might perform with honour in their classes (or in events where a handicap-strewn marking system might sometimes favour them), but no other model was likely to have the straight-line performance, the potentially rugged strength, and the sheer versatility to fight for victories.

Looking into the crystal ball in 1957, as far as BMC was concerned, the only possible in-house rival to the 100-Six was the forthcoming MG MGA Twin-Cam, but as this was not due for launch until mid-1958, and had only a 108bhp/1.6-litre engine; it did not seem to have the potential of the Big Healey.

Out in the wide world, a big, broad-shouldered, 2.6-litre Healey would have to compete against exotica like the Mercedes-Benz 300SL (which, when properly prepared, was a surprisingly rugged though exotically-specified rally car), but it also had to compete against the nimble, high-revving Alfa Romeo Guilietta coupes, and the rock-solid twin-cam Carrera-engined Porsche 356s.

Not only that, but it also had to face up to the works

Triumph TR3s. However, for BMC the good news was that the Triumph team seemed incapable, or unwilling, to go in for any performance-enhancing development programmes, for its factory rally cars were no faster, and no better, than privately-owned examples. The management team was smug, and could not see why faster cars were necessary – but as the Healey continued to improve as season followed season, it would soon find out why.

In the mid-1950s, when the 100-Six was conceived, European rallies had settled down into two main categories. One was the type which used sealed asphalt surfaces, almost entirely on public highways – either speed hillclimbs in the mountains of such favourably blessed countries like France, Italy or Austria, or tightly-timed road sections on twisty minor roads.

The French Alpine (whose target schedules were persistently being raised) was already teetering on the edge of being anti-social as far as other road users were concerned, for it was run off in high summer, on some of the most picturesque roads in the Alps. Other events – like the Dutch Tulip (whose open-road speed sections were never in Holland!) – played it safe by mainly using speed hillclimb tests where the public could be kept away, with a relatively relaxed road section between them. The Monte Carlo Rally (still hugely prestigious because of the publicity it gained) was a special case because in January it was almost bound to be run on snow and ice, though under all the white stuff there was invariably a French public highway!

On the other hand, the trend was for other rallies to use loose surfaces, and to combine them with speed tests. Although Liège-Rome-Liège was still mainly a tarmac endurance event in the late 1950s, every year more and more loose/rough-road sections were being included to the route – the 1958 event, which struck deeply into Yugoslavia (and, incidentally, went nowhere near Rome!), being a case in point.

It was in Scandinavia that rallies tended to run more and more on loose, gravel-strewn, surfaces. Not only did the local drivers (Gunnar Andersson/Volvo was already a

Abingdon – the home of the works rally team

In the beginning, the Pavlova Works at Abingdon, just a few miles south of Oxford, produced leather goods, but had become disused by 1929 when William Morris bought it as the site of his fast-expanding MG sports car business. For the next half century – until 1980, when the very last MG MGB was assembled there – it was not only MG's home, but also the home of the Austin Healey brand from 1957.

Expanded piecemeal, especially during and after the Second World War, the site eventually had a melange of old, quite old, and new-but-basic buildings. When the BMC Competitions Department was formally set up at the end of 1954, with Marcus Chambers as its manager, the competition cars were prepared in one corner of the site. Although the department moved once, in the early days, there was never any other upheaval, and no more than modest modernisation, even though the cars became progressively more high-tech.

'Comps' relied on the mainstream factory for some services (such as paintwork rectification, and some trim work), but was otherwise self-contained: it was years – into the 1960s, even – before an engine rolling road was installed.

At its peak, the Abingdon production plant was churning out up to 1000 cars a week. In the 1970s, however, British Leyland's policies did it no favours, the surge of British sterling against the American dollar also hit hard, and by 1979 every MG produced there was making a financial loss. Assembly closed down, the site was stripped, sold off to property developers, razed to the ground, and is now totally submerged under a mass of new industrial buildings.

Every trace of the famous old 'Comps' department has been lost.

star combination, and Erik Carlsson/Saab was about to join in ...) have the expertise to allow them to teeter on the edge of grip at all times, they also developed new techniques to take account of such tracks. Until and unless BMC had such drivers (and it was still wedded to using all-British crews – a policy which would not change until 1962), and a car which could cope with gravel stages, it would be at a disadvantage.

On the other hand, once Marcus Chambers' team at Abingdon got stuck into a Big Healey development programme, they set a precedent that was an example to all other teams, though most would not follow suit for years. Subject to the budgets always being available (and, in this period, there never seemed to be a shortage of funds to finance an ambitious programme) development could go ahead on a long term basis.

It seems that BMC's enthusiasts (Marcus Chambers, Geoff Healey, John Gott and Douggie Watts, in particular) used to sit down regularly to work out how the Healey could be further enhanced – whereas most of their competitors were happy enough to potter on with the model which was already being built.

Not only did they work out what "freedoms" (as the English translation of the homologation *Blue Book* so quaintly put it) were available, but how they could take advantage of them. Which other teams, for instance, equipped their cars with all aluminium skin panels, four-wheel disc brakes, alternative cylinder heads, and alternative carburation and exhaust manifolds – all of which were sporting-legal at this time?

The result, which took years to evolve, but which became gloriously obvious by 1962 when the first Weber-carburettor-equipped Healey went rallying, was that the Healey 3000 became the sport's very first Group 3 'homologation special'. Every performance-raising item which was allowed was specified, every optional extra which had to sell in small numbers was made available, and every advantage was taken of the allowances written in the still-vague regulations. By 1962/63 a works Big Healey was formidably better – both faster and stronger – than the road cars which were still being sold in large numbers: at a time when road cars had 132bhp, a works car had 210bhp – plus different transmission, different bodywork, and a mountain of different detailing.

The Big Healey – mountain master

By the time that much of the development work had come to fruition (particularly after the aluminium cylinder head/triple Weber carburettor installation had matured), the Healey was a formidable tarmac rally car which, by nature of its great strength, was also a real contender on rough events where sheer structural strength was an asset.

Much testing work on race tracks, and in private special stage development, had turned the road car (which was too low slung and not well-balanced enough) into a better balanced, though heavy, high-speed missile. Although it could be argued that only one driver – Timo Makinen – truly mastered every aspect of the Healey's chassis, Don Morley and Pat Moss both eventually came close.

In a straight line (and up-hill) it also became a very fast car. In 1958 the original works 100-Six models were really no faster than the 2.2-litre Triumph TR3As of the day (as French Alpine Rally results showed), but within four years they had the beating of every rally car – except occasionally the 300SL, or perhaps a truly 'hot' Carrera-engined Porsche 356.

Later, in 1965, when the Healey was coming to the end of its rally career, I was working with *Autocar* magazine, and had the pleasure of driving the Morley twins' ex-French Alpine car (DRX 258C) for a full week. Along with Geoffrey Howard, not only did I take performance figures, but I used it for commuting, and finally delivered it back to Abingdon. At the time (and, I must say, ever since) this qualified as one of the highlights of my motoring life.

The performance was astonishing. Although it reached only 120mph (that was because it was geared-down for pass-storming in the French Alps with a 4.30:1 instead of a 3.91:1 final drive ratio) it sprinted from 0-60mph in 8.2 seconds, and to 100mph in 19.2 seconds. By the standards of the day this was Jaguar E-Type performance, and it quite obliterated whatever the standard Healey 3000 BJ8 road car could achieve.

Not only that, but there always seemed to the right gear for every occasion. Overdrive was fitted, and available on top and third gears, the switch actually being located on the gear lever knob, and the engine soared easily up to 6000rpm, though a strict rev limit was imposed on us at that level. With three big Webers gobbling away up front, maybe that explains why the overall fuel consumption we measured was 13.7mpg, but at the time none of us cared a jot. By the standards of the day, this was still the ultimate British tarmac rally car – and we could quite see why the Morleys had won two French Alpine rallies, and set fastest stages times on four consecutive Tulips into the bargain.

Facing up to rival cars

When the Austin Healey 100-Six started its rallying career in 1958, no serious works team had yet worked out that careful homologation could lead to the evolution of a very specialised rally car. In addition, since the majority of Europe's most significant rallies were still being held on tarmac or, at least, on hard surfaces, there was as yet little need to develop a car where the ability to scrabble around on gravel surfaces was important.

Although the works Big Healey was probably the first to evolve over the years as a special-purpose rally (and to a lesser degree race) car, this only happened slowly in the first two seasons, Accordingly, I should list its major rivals from the late 1950s, then mention those which appeared in the early 1960s:

Alfa Romeo Giulietta SZ – front engine/rear-drive. The lightest/fiercest derivative of this Italian car, with a 100bhp/1.3-litre twin-cam engine, and five-speed transmission. Great handling, surprisingly reliable, and with its small engine, sometimes favoured by handicapping formulae. Had already won the French Alpine and Liège-Rome-Liège rallies outright.

The last of the 'Morley Healeys' was DRX 258C, which the author used for a week during the summer of 1965. The fascia of the BJ8 was much tidier than that of earlier works Healeys, and featured an overdrive switch on the gearlever knob.

Mercedes-Benz 300 SL – front-engine/rear-drive. First used in 1954. According to the statistics, one of the fastest cars in the world, but could be rather fragile when faced with tough conditions. Handling required learning. When driven by serious competitors – such as Olivier Gendebien and Walter Shock – could be a rally winner. The drawback was that the factory was not really interested in rallying.

Porsche 356 and Carrera – rear-engine/rear-drive. First used in early-1950s, but engines gradually enlarged over time. Very solidly built, usually very reliable, but with tail-happy handling. Superb traction made it competitive on all types of surface. Could be ultra-competitive where the twin-cam Carrera engines were used.

Triumph TR3/TR3A – front-engine/rear-drive. First used in 1954 (then as a TR2), in a very competitive works team, let down by a lack of engine power development, so 2.2-litres/100bhp was rarely exceeded. Over time, performance stagnated, while that of the Healeys soared ahead.

Sunbeam Rapier – front-engine/rear-drive. First used in 1956, a triumph of development and team organisation over basic design. Brave drivers like Peter Harper and Paddy Hopkirk made up for a lack of power – 90bhp/1.6-litres in saloon form was barely sufficient.

As season followed season, we should really add:

Alfa Romeo Giulia TZ – front-engine/rear-drive. First used in 1963, further evolution of the SZ theme, now with 1.6-litres/130bhp, a lighter chassis, all-independent suspension and disc brakes. Looked fragile, but could be an outright winner on tarmac.

BMC Mini Cooper S – front-engine/front-drive. First used in 1962 (as the Mini Cooper), a rival from within the same workshops as the Big Healey! When fully developed, with 110bhp/1.3-litres, magnificent handling and the same team of drivers, was phenomenally fast and versatile. Not quite as rapid on tarmac, but near unbeatable on loose or low-grip surfaces.

Ford Cortina GT and Lotus-Cortina – front-engine/rear-drive. First used in 1963, originally with 100bhp/1.5-litre overhead-valve engines then (from 1965 in regular works form) with 150bhp/1.6-litre twin-cam engines. Fragile until developed by the works team, but better in the loose than the Big Healey.

Porsche 911 – rear-engine/rear-drive. First used in 1965, with no more than 160bhp/2.0-litres. Porsche was more committed to motor racing than rallying, but with the right drivers (Vic Elford from 1967, Bjorn Waldegård from 1968/69) there was so much still to come. Strong, and with superb traction, it could have annihilated the Big Healey.

Homologation – meeting the rules

For more than 50 years, cars have only been able to compete in top-class rallies if they have been 'homologated' in accordance with the FIA's criteria (or, in the case of British teams, via the RAC) – in other words, if they have been approved for use.

Although the first full text of Appendix J of the *International Sporting Code* came into force in February 1955, it was some time before the process of homologation was regularised, with detail specification forms, figures and photographs all applying to a particular car. The tightening of Appendix J was necessary because (nothing new here ...) some drivers and teams were happy to cheat if they could get away with it.

Appendix J was further revised for 1957, and again for 1958, this being the first year in which Homologation Forms were issued. From that time, homologated rally cars could run in these categories:

Group 1: Production saloon cars with four passenger seats, of which 5000 had to be built. Virtually no modifications were allowed.

Group 2: Production saloon cars, with four seats, of which 1000 had to be built. If manufacturers proved that an equivalent number of parts or kits had been sold, many other modifications could be made.

Big Healeys being assembled at Abingdon in the late 1950s – note the MGAs, the Twin-Cams, and the frog-eye Sprites in the same group.

Group 3: Production sports cars with two seats, of which 500 had to be built. The same allowance regarding parts and kits as Group 2 also applied.

There were other groups – 4, 5, and 6 – which did not usually apply to rallying at that time.

To 'prove' that the minimum number of cars had been built, the FIA required a solemn written statement from a senior executive of the company concerned [in the case of the Healey, I understand that this was John Thornley, general manager of the MG Car Co, at Abingdon, where the Big Healey was assembled]. In those days there was no

Front disc brakes were finally adopted for the Austin Healey 3000 in 1959.

question of production claims being verified, or queried, either by the FIA, or by a team's rivals, and inspections were therefore unknown. Most manufacturers played the game, up to a point, but all were ready to push credibility to the limits, to get a new model into rallying as swiftly as possible.

The Healey, naturally, ran in Group 3, and in that group the basic provisions to Appendix J (French, incidentally, was the 'official language', as the FIA was based in Paris, so one always had to be cautious regarding translations) allowed several important extra freedoms.

Naturally, it was always permitted to beef up the structure by welding, and by plating, it was possible to fit different-material body panels to all outer skin panels (but not to the basic structure itself), and every manufacturer was allowed to specify an alternative carburation system to whatever was standard at the time. A whole range of extra equipment could be homologated if at least 100 such items or kits had been sold – which explains why aluminium

instead of cast iron cylinder heads, gearbox and axle casings could be used, and why items like disc brake kits and oil coolers could be approved eventually.

Gaining homologation for the Big Healey was always straightforward, not only because the basic car was always in serious series production, but because many of the optional extras genuinely sold in significant quantities.

Because between 4000 and 7000 six-cylinder engined Healeys were being produced in every calendar year throughout the late-1950s and the 1960s, there was never any difficulty in convincing the FIA that a minimum of 500 cars of each type had been produced. For example, when BMC began rallying the 100-Six in 1958, more than 7000 cars had already been produced, and when the first of the 3000s followed in mid-1959, well over 1000 cars had been produced (and shipped to North America) before the new model was even introduced to the public.

Now for a description of assembly sources. From 1956 until the late autumn of 1957, the 100-Six was always assembled at the vast BMC (Austin, actually) factory at Longbridge, in the southern outskirts of Birmingham. Then, from the autumn of 1957 (there being a slight overlap with Longbridge production, which took time to tail off), assembly was transferred to the MG sports car factory at Abingdon, near Oxford, where it remained until the end of Big Healey production in 1967/68, long after the Healey had been retired from rallying.

Although it was team manager Marcus Chambers himself who looked after homologation for the early cars, it was the youthful Bill Price, who joined him as a lowly assistant, who shouldered the burden ever afterwards. As Bill once told me: "When I started at Abingdon in 1960, Marcus Chambers said to me on my very first day: 'I've got a little job you can do – look after all the homologation forms.' So, from that day until the Department closed in 1970, I was responsible for acquiring the info, collating the forms, and getting them off to the RAC. We did manage to incorporate one or two 'fiddles' during this time ..."

But no big ones. It was Geoff Healey, after all, who had already made sure that four-wheel disc brakes were

Building and homologating the 3000

Unlike some other cars covered in this series of books, there was never any problem in building and selling enough cars to gain homologation. Except for some of the so-called 'optional extras' (the four-wheel disc brake kits, and the aluminium cylinder heads were perfect examples), the cars were built in large quantities, such that no rival could possibly complain that sporting homologation had been rushed, or somehow fiddled.

For the record, the first 20 Austin Healey 100 (BN1) cars were assembled by the Healey Motor Co. Ltd., at Warwick, but true series production began at Longbridge in mid-1953, where the cars took shape in a dedicated hall. The BN1, the BN2 and (until late 1957) the 100-Six BN4, were all assembled at Longbridge, while the ultra-specialised 100S (a race car which really forms no part of this story) was assembled at Warwick.

Assembly of 100-Six models was then transferred to the MG sports car factory at Abingdon in the late autumn of 1957, which means that BN4, BN6, BN7, and BJ8s of all types were assembled there, just a few yards away from the works Competitions Department. The last series of BJ8s was produced before the end of 1967, with a single BJ8 produced, from available spare parts, in the spring of 1968.

Every single chassis/inner structure for this long-lived family of cars was manufactured by Jensen Motors of West Bromwich, in the West Midlands, the shells also painted and partly trimmed at West Bromwich before they were transported to one or other of the final assembly factories.

The following figures tell the story of a car which was not only a sporting, but also a commercial success:

Model	Years produced	Numbers produced
100/4 (BN1)	1953-55	10,030
100S	1955	50
100/4 (BN2)	1955-56	404
100-Six BN4/BN6	1956-59	15,444
3000 MkI BN7/BT7	1959-61	13,650
3000 MkII BN7/BT7	1961-62	5451
3000 MkII Conv. BJ7	1962-63	6113
3000 MkIII Conv BJ8	1964-68	16,322

Between 1957 (when the rally programme began) to 1965 (when it ended), six-cylinder Austin Healey production fluctuated between approximately 4000 and 8000 a year. Since homologation requirements were for only 500 mechanically-identical cars to be built, this was obviously no problem for Abingdon and its planners.

approved as 'optional equipment' on all six-cylinder models. After that, almost every other change (such as providing the humped GRP boot lid, altering the bodywork to provide external access to the twin-choke Weber carburettors, and reshuffling the structure to allow the exhaust silencers to be carried in a higher location) was done after a very careful reading of the Appendix J regulations. Not only was Bill Price adept at this, but his second boss (from 1961), Stuart Turner, could have given lessons on tactics to Machiavelli ... Unlike other manufacturers, BMC rarely needed to take exceptional measures (for which, read 'questionable tactics') to get improvements to the Healey approved. As the road car changed, so did the rally car – and both were all the better for that.

Engineering features

One reason that the Healey was always such a solid rally car was the way that its structure was designed around much of the Austin A90 running gear. Even when the original 100/4 was being engineered in 1951/52, Geoff Healey and his small team made sure that this was not just another conventional sports car, with a chassis frame and separate body shell.

Instead, they designed what was, in effect, a steel platform chassis, to which the entire steel inner structure of a two-seater sports car was to be welded (not bolted) during original build. The passenger bulkhead, the inner wing pressings (front and rear), and the front cross panels between the front suspension areas – all of them steel panels – were all attached at this stage, and all were jigged up, then welded together, at Jensen in West Bromwich.

Every skin panel, the doors and some of the outer structure came later in that assembly process – but (unlike other sports cars like the MG MGA or the TR2) it meant that in future years there was never any question of renovating a crashed or otherwise careworn car with a new chassis frame – an entire new chassis/inner structure would be needed instead.

This, then, was the basis of the Big Healey, a solidly-engineered, solidly-built inner structure which would prove, again and again, just how rugged it was going to be as a competition car. Works and private owners all had good reason to be happy about that, though mechanics who had

Top: This front end view of a Healey body/chassis structure restoration shows its complexity.

Middle: Austin Healey chassis frames were welded to inner panels on initial assembly, which meant that crash repairs could be complex and lengthy. This particular car, in fact, is a four-cylinder example, but the basic structure did not change over the years.

Right: These were the complete Austin Healey chassis/underframe/inner panels as completed at Jensen (here restored for a 'classic' life).

The very first Austin Healey rolling chassis, as completed in 1952, showing the platform chassis construction, with the main chassis members passing under the line of the rear axle.

to tackle rebuilds – and restorers who had to rejuvenate rusty wrecks after years of abuse – found that a lot of effort was needed to keep the cars in good condition.

If there was a fundamental design error – and yes, I will now suggest that it was an unfortunate error – it was the decision to make the platform frame very simple (to keep down the expense of press tooling), with straight 'chassis' side members, and to have them pass underneath the line of the solid rear axle. Also as on the Healey's major rival – the TR2/TR3/TR3A/TR4 – this meant that, by definition,

rear axle movement was unduly restricted, and that the rear-end ground clearance was always restricted.

Dynamically, too, there was a tendency for the rear axle to pick up an inside wheel on sharp corners, and for traction to be lost. An optional limited-slip differential would eventually alleviate this failing, but it meant that in certain conditions rally cars like the 300SL, the Porsche Carrera and the Alfa Romeo Giulia TZ (all of which had independent rear suspension) had a definite advantage.

For perfectly good commercial reasons, the original

four-speed manual transmission and rear axle as used by saloon cars like the new-generation A90 Westminster and Wolseley 6/90 types.

The six-cylinder engine was a big, heavy, straight 'six' with iron cylinder block and head castings. Originally of 2639cc, the design was always provided with a little bit of capacity 'stretch', so when the Healey 3000 came along it was enlarged to 2912cc – and for motorsport purposes that could be further increased to something close to the 3-litre capacity class limit.

The original engine, as fitted to the BN4, had simply awful breathing arrangements, for the 'inlet manifold' was no more than a gallery cast into the head itself, with carburettors bolted on to that head. The exhaust port breathing was better, but not much better – the result being an engine which was almost impervious to power-tuning, which made it useless for motorsport purposes.

Happily, from the autumn of 1957, the 100-Six was provided with a much-revised engine, incorporating a new (still cast iron) head casting with six proper inlet ports and enlarged passages. With this equipped, road car power went up from 102bhp to 117bhp, and characters like Geoff Healey and Eddie Maher (of the BMC Engines branch in Coventry) soon discovered that this had become an eminently tuneable power unit. By the time the works Healey 3000s came along in 1959, they had well over 150bhp, and by the time the last of the three-SU engines were used in 1961 they had 180bhp.

100/4 Type BN1 of 1952 had been engineered around the major engine, transmission, front suspension and steering pieces from BMC's existing Austin A90 Atlantic. It was to encourage use of these pieces that BMC's chairman, Leonard Lord, had allowed Healey to do this, and it was an obvious factor in his decision to take over a 'Healey' and turn it into an 'Austin Healey'.

Even before the original Austin Healey went into series production in 1953, a ruthless process of rationalisation had already begun at BMC. One result was that old and existing 'building blocks' used in the BN1 were soon swept away, to be replaced by a new generation of what were known as C-Series engines, transmissions and axles. The result was that when the slightly longer-wheelbase 100-Six was introduced in mid-1956, it had the same basic six-cylinder engine,

For the first few years, all six-cylinder Healeys used a modified version of the modern C-Series four-speed gearbox, with Laycock overdrive as optional equipment. Until Marcus Chambers and his team got to work on the homologation of special items, the ratios were none too special, and the gearbox casing was arranged to have its selectors at the side (this was to make steering-column change easier to arrange on saloons which used the same box). That explains, too, why the 100-Six and earlier 3000s had a cranked, direct-acting gearlever located at the left side of the gearbox. Overdrive, where fitted, operated on top and third gears.

At the front end, much of the coil spring independent front suspension was lifted straight out of the BMC C-Series parts bin, as was the cam and peg steering, though spring rates and lever-arm damper settings were altered to suit the lighter sports car.

As far as the body shell was concerned, by the time the 100-Six was introduced, almost the entire body shell was built from pressed steel, the doors still had removable plastic side screens, and the rather bulbous (but distinctive) hard-top was still an optional extra.

It was, in other words, an absolutely typical and conventional British sports cars of the late 1950s variety. The big difference, though, was that it was rallied by a truly determined works team, which discovered ways of making it faster, more versatile, and more solidly-built than could ever have been envisaged when it was new.

Motorsport development, and improvements

Before going into detail about the improvements which were progressively made to the structure and running gear of these cars, it is important to chart the change in the Big Healey's appearance, and specification over the years.

Each and every works rally car was used in hard-top condition – one reason being the overall aerodynamic package was improved in this way, the other being that it was felt that this would provide a modicum of extra safety in case the car was rolled. Subsequent experience showed that the hard-top was quick to collapse when the weight of an inversion pressed down upon it, but thankfully no one was ever seriously injured in a roll-over accident.

Although such fitments have subsequently been used on cars entered in classic racing, no works Healey, by the way, was ever fitted with a roll cage, however rudimentary, in the 1960s. In those days such fitments were never even considered, and when the first examples were fitted to other race cars in the early 1960s (a USA-built Ford Galaxie was one of the first to be submitted in 1963), event scrutineers tended to reject them on the grounds that they were stiffening up the structure!

Apart from the usual use of extra driving lamps, the original works 100-Six cars looked positively normal and all, without exception, used centre-lock wire-spoke wheels: all subsequent works Healeys used such wheels until the end of the car's career in 1965. The final car prepared to take part in the 1967 RAC Rally ran on centre-lock Minilite wheels, but since this car was due to run in the prototype category, this was an obvious exception.

Then came the changes, which were made so gradually that each car seemed to differ only slightly from its predecessors. Apart from acknowledging that front and rear bumpers were sometimes fitted, and sometimes not (this was done to take advantage of specific regulations which applied to individual events, and to the classes which the cars ran in, which sometimes allowed lightening to take place), it should also be noted that similar regulations allowed the full width front grille to be trimmed, or even removed.

Although every road-car version of the six-cylinder Healey (100-Six and 3000) ran with a complete chrome-plated front grille filling the aperture, works rally cars often looked startlingly different, this being done to allow even more cooling air to enter the engine bay, and incidentally to find its way towards the front wheelarches and the hard-used brakes.

In fact, works rally cars first ran without full-width radiator grilles in the French Alpine Rally of 1958, where ambient temperatures in high summer were high, the original grilles being rather crudely chopped out at the sides of the aperture. It was on the same event, incidentally, that

The rear end of a fully-developed Austin Healey 3000 rally car, complete with rear-wheel disc brakes, 14-leaf suspension springs, enlarged lever-arm dampers, and an alloy casing for the rear axle final drive.

To allow the boot to contain a large fuel tank, and two spare wheels, Abingdon eventually developed this re-shaped boot lid, which did nothing for the styling, but was an immensely practical fitting.

they ran without bumpers, and with low-mounted extra driving lamps. However, because detail regulations differed from event to event, even as late as 1960 they could still sometimes be seen with standard full-width grilles.

Side exhaust pipe outlets (under the passenger door) were first seen in 1959, this system being arranged so that tail pipes did not have to go all the way to the back of the car, and be taken under the line of the axle, and below the line of the main chassis members, as they did on production-line built cars. Not only did this save a significant amount of weight, but it also eliminated the possibility of that part of the exhaust system being damaged, or flattened, by the rough roads which were an increasing part of the current rally scene.

For 1960, a cockpit cooling scoop was fitted to the

scuttle ahead of the base of the windscreen, though this never seemed to be as efficient as it promised to be.

Later, the characteristically shaped, moulded glass-fibre boot lid (which allowed two spare wheels to be carried inside the shallow boot) was first used on cars built for the French Alpine Rally of 1960. This proved to be so useful that it was immediately standardised in the specification, for Appendix J regulations allowed such a non-functional change to be made without insisting that minimum quantities had to be sold first.

From mid-1960, too, a simple air vent flap was fitted to the rear of the hard-tops, just ahead of the line of the rear window, this aiming to reduce the sometimes searing heat inside the cockpit. Romantics would hope that these were specially designed, but the truth is more prosaic – they

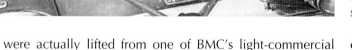

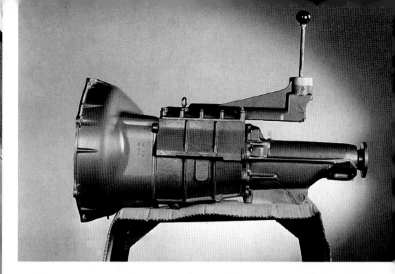

The last, and by far the most satisfactory, gearbox layout on the Austin Healey 3000 was this type, with a remote-control change. This was standard from 1962 to the end of production in 1967-68.

From 1962, triple dual-choke Weber carburettors were homologated for the Austin Healey 3000 – and were a tight fit under the bonnet of the standard-style car. To ease access, an extra removable panel was let in to the shroud panel above the carburettors.

were actually lifted from one of BMC's light-commercial vehicles!

The next visual change occurred in May 1961, when cars for the Tulip Rally featured hot air outlets in the front wings, behind the wheelarch cut outs. Freely acknowledged to have been copies from those used in the Mercedes-Benz 300SL (and finalised after a good deal of ad hoc open-road testing), these helped maintain a cooling flow of air in the engine bay: since a six-branch fabricated exhaust manifold had recently been adopted, temperatures were significantly higher than before. Apparently these vents (which were fitted to both sides of the car, of course), were developed by cut-and-test methods by Abingdon technician Cliff Humphries.

There was more to come. From the first few months of 1962, new Big Healeys in the 37-77ARX sequence were fitted with a long, slim, detachable panel in the bonnet surround (the shroud, as some experts call it) on the left (passenger/co-driver) side of the car. This first appeared on the Tulip Rally of 1962, to coincide with the introduction of engines using twin-choke Weber carburettors, and was intended to allow easy access to those instruments, which were immediately under that point of the bodywork. This modification was retro-fitted to many older Healeys when they were later fitted with Webers.

Extra headlamps, in nacelles ('frog-eye' Sprite-style) let in to the bonnet shroud on each side, and just ahead of the bonnet opening, were first seen on the 1962 RAC Rally. They were only intermittently seen on cars in 1963, but became a standard feature on all cars prepared for the

1964 and 1965 seasons. These were fitted to provide a conventional headlamp dipping facility, for it was at this time the main headlamps had been fitted with Lucas quartz-halogen bulbs, which were only originally available in single-filament form.

The very first works cars to have wind-up windows and the wrap-around windscreen were the 1964-built BJ8s (ARX 91B and ARX 92B), and of course the final cars also built in 1964 and 1965 (BMO 93B, BRX 852B, DRX 257C, DRX 258C and EJB 806C). Because of yet another reshuffle of FIA Appendix J regulations, those cars were usually obliged to run with front and rear bumpers in place (though not on the 'bring-anything-you've-got' Spa-Sofia-Liège marathon, where BMO 93B won outright in old-fashioned, no-bumper condition).

Except for the never-rallied 1967 prototype car (for the RAC Rally, which was cancelled less than 24-hours before the start), the very last visual change came in the autumn of 1965 (for the RAC Rally – as it happened, the very last event which a works Healey was to start) when two cars – DRX 258C and the brand-new EJB 806C – were equipped with high-exhaust installations under a shortened passenger door. This involved a major carve-up of the inner structure, at the front end, of the bulkhead, of the lower body sill, and, of course, of the passenger door itself.

Structural changes

The original rally cars of 1957 and 1958 relied mostly on the natural strength of the existing Healey Motor Co. design, and on the integrity of the structures which had been welded together by Jensen at West Bromwich. It was only after the battering sustained by the cars in the Liège-Rome-Liège of 1958 was observed, and analysed, that progressive strengthening was carried out on subsequent cars.

Because the main box-section chassis frame was welded up to the steel inner body structure on initial manufacture at Jensen, it was impossible for the mechanics at Abingdon to carry out a total strip-down to a 'chassis only' condition. Even so, after every tough event, as much as possible of the car – its outer skin panels, its doors, its hard-top, and, of course, all its running gear, were taken off for refurbishment and repair.

As the later team manager Peter Browning has commented: "Certain cars were individually developed over quite a long period ... Unlike the works Minis, very few Healeys were re-bodied to appear again, perhaps with new registration numbers. Generally, the cars kept their identity and were rebuilt, some albeit upon new chassis frames. Once a works Healey was pensioned off, it was either written off (the chassis being too badly damaged to be of use) or, if the car was still basically sound, it would be sold to a private owner ..."

As the years progressed, strengthening panels or reinforcements were added on the front cross-member, to beef up the front (lever arm type) shock absorber mountings, around the steering box mounting brackets, under and around the rear of the chassis frame, and where larger Armstrong rear shock absorbers had to be supported.

In addition, with rough events like the Liège, or RAC rallies, in mind, a considerable amount of extra plating would be added to the underside of the main chassis members, and, of course, the skid shielding under the engine and gearbox would itself be very strong.

Engine

When Abingdon first began using the 100-Six, the 2639cc engine was rated at 117bhp, and virtually no optional equipment was homologated for the car. Even when the 3000 was homologated in mid-1959, the 2912cc engines were only equipped with two SU carburettors on a special inlet manifold, and we may guess (though nothing was revealed at the time) that they had about 160bhp.

For 1960, however, and strictly according to the FIA's 'freedoms', an alternative carburation system was homologated – this being three 2in SU H8 carburettors – and it was with this engine, which produced up to 180bhp, that Pat Moss and Ann Wisdom recorded that amazing outright victory in the Liège-Rome-Liège Rally of September 1960. A six-branch tubular exhaust manifold was added to the specification from early 1961, this also

C-Series engines

No sooner had the British Motor Corporation (BMC) been set up in 1952, than work began on new engine families for full corporate use, including a conventional straight 'six', called the C-Series, which would eventually be built in 2.6 and 2.9-litre form, and would go into a whole variety of BMC family cars, sports cars and even commercial vehicles. Over the years, it was used in cars like the Austin A99/A110, the Vanden Plas Princess 3-litre, the Morris Isis, and in several BMC commercial vehicles.

Equipped with a cast iron block and cast iron cylinder head, with a four-bearing crankshaft, the original 2639cc engine was inflicted with an awful cylinder head, in which the inlet manifold was cast into the head in the form of a gallery, and in the case of the original BN4, with two SU carburettors bolted direct to the head casting.

As far as competition cars were concerned, no amount of work could make this engine breathe properly, which was a dead loss as far as Abingdon was concerned. However, when the revised engine came along in late 1957, complete with a new head casting, proper inlet passages, and the chance to fit alternative instruments (like Webers, eventually), things immediately looked up, and the Big Healey's march toward 200+bhp power outputs in rally car form began.

Although the aluminium cylinder head was homologated in 1962, this was only ever available as optional equipment, and as far as is known, no production line-built Healey 3000 was ever so equipped.

As far as production line engines were concerned, raw castings were always sourced from specialist suppliers. All machining and assembly was then completed at the BMC Engines Branch factory in Courthouse Green, Coventry, after which Healey engines were delivered to Longbridge (1954-57), or to Abingdon (1957-67) by the truck load.

adding a small, but unspecified, increase in torque and, perhaps, peak power.

The next big change came early in 1962, when BMC not only re-homologated its rally car on the basis of the 3000 MkII (which had its own, very different, three-SU installation) but employed the 'alternative carburation' freedom to homologate a triple dual-choke Weber carburettor installation. This was the moment at which an aluminium cylinder head was also homologated. Now, according to the regulations, BMC should already have sold 100 such heads by the time approval followed, which it most assuredly had not, but none of its rivals ever complained in case some of their transgressions were picked up and paraded against them!

The combination of Webers-plus-aluminium cylinder produced a very torquey 210bhp, and saw the C-Series engine at the peak of its development, for no further major improvements were made in the 1962-65 period.

If ultimate power, rather than a four-day/multi-thousand-mile endurance tune was required, then more power could have been produced – and was, indeed, produced for circuit racing by the Warwick-based race team – but since Abingdon was determined to produce engines which would (theoretically, at least) easily last through a major international rally, this does not seem to have been done. Although rev-limiters were not fitted, the drivers were always instructed to use 6000rpm as the absolute limit. The only recurrent, infuriating, and seemingly random failure which seemed to occur was that Lucas electrical distributors were still failing as much in the mid-1960s, as they had been in 1959!

Transmissions

Each and every works Big Healey used the same basic cast iron gearbox casing as the road cars of the period, the same basic A-Type Laycock overdrive (which featured epicyclic gearing, electric actuation control via a solenoid and, on late-model cars, an actuation switch fixed to the gear lever itself), and the same massive C-Series back axle.

Several different sets of internal gearbox ratios were eventually homologated, the close ratio set which was favoured being what is now known as the 'Tulip Rally' set. A limited-slip differential was finally used from 1963 (it let down the Morley twins' car on the Alpine Rally of that year), and several different final drive ratios were also made available.

Was the Big Healey unique?

In that it was the very first 'homologation special' to be developed for motorsport, the Healey was certainly unique. If BMC had been extremely profitable (which it was not, at the time), and totally committed to motorsport at the time (which, by comparison with companies like Ford, it was not), then it would no doubt have put even more effort into the evolution of the cars than it did.

In the late 1950s, no other car manufacturer carried out such a lengthy and determined development programme for a rally car – one which turned a conventional sports car into a very special motorsport machine – and it was not until 1963, and the arrival of three other new models – the Ford Lotus-Cortina, the Alfa Romeo Giulia TI Super, and the BMC Mini Cooper S – that the company was matched in its intent.

Where the Healey was certainly unique was that, by this development process, so much was achieved from profoundly discouraging beginnings. I can think of no other concern which could have taken a low-slung and asthmatic motor car (the original 102bhp 100-Six) and turned it into a near-unbreakable, fire-breathing, 210bhp rally winner in only five years. Not only did the engine become twice as powerful while being enlarged by just 10 per cent, but the car's structure itself was turned into something akin to a two-seater tank.

Building and running the works cars

In the beginning, BMC could see little future for Austin Healeys with four-cylinder engines, for they lacked ground clearance, and development potential. Even so, much initial motorsport development was carried out by the Donald Healey Motor Co. at Warwick, either for racing

Aluminium panels

Almost the entire skin of a works Healey 3000 was made up of aluminium panels, whereas most of the skin of the production car was made of pressed steel. Aluminium, of course, was employed as a weight reduction measure, and according to a reading of the Group 3 homologation regulations which applied up to the end of 1965, this was a totally sporting-legal substitution.

The English translation of the official French text stated that the material of any panel 'licked by the air stream' could be changed, which therefore meant any skin panel, though the inference was that no inner panels, bulkheads or stiffeners could be changed.

As far as is known, in all cases, the BMC works body structures (or complete cars, in many cases) arrived at Abingdon with normal steel panels. In the process of preparation, however, a series of aluminium panels were fitted instead, these having been ordered through Jensen and Boulton Paul, who would occasionally run off small numbers of aluminium panels on the same presses that normally produced pressed steel.

Although I have never seen documentary evidence of how much weight was saved by such substitutions, I am prepared to believe that it was in excess of 68kg/150lb. As one age-old motor-racing sage once quoted, it is always best to "simplicate [sic] and add lightness" – and most observers would also agree that it was cheaper to save weight than to tune the engine to make the same difference in power/weight ratio.

(such as the Le Mans 24-hour race), or for endurance record runs in the USA. Geoff Healey was the calm and extremely experienced guiding genius behind all this work.

When the 100-Six was introduced in 1956, prospects for the latest car improved considerably, especially when a new type of cylinder head showed just how much potential was still locked inside. The very first factory-backed six-cylinder Healeys were race and record cars, all of them being prepared at the cramped and old-fashioned Healey Motor Co. factory in Warwick.

It was only in 1958, when Marcus Chambers decided that the Healey was the only existing (and planned) BMC model that might eventually provide him with a potential outright-winning rally car, that work began on building a team of cars at Abingdon.

After the Monte Carlo Rally of 1958, Geoff Healey handed over the single 100-Six (UOC 741) which had already been used in international rallies, together with all the records and expertise that could be amassed, and left Abingdon to get on with it. Thereafter, Abingdon would build every works rally Healey (and would turn the occasional rally car into a race car, too), while Warwick would only build cars for use in endurance races, such as the Le Mans 24-hour, and Sebring (USA) 12-hour events.

This, in fact, made a great deal of practical sense – not only because the expertise were therefore being concentrated in sensible areas, but because by that time every Austin Healey road car was being assembled at Abingdon, from painted/trimmed/wired body chassis units provided from Jensen in West Bromwich.

To someone who was used to visiting many works competition departments at this time, Abingdon was different from most of the others. Not only did the cars take shape in a big workshop (at least 15, perhaps more, cars were sometimes crammed into one area), but Healeys, Mini Coopers, MGAs and MGBs, and a whole variety of other models all jostled for space.

Marcus Chambers (and later Stuart Turner) ran the department from a first-floor office overlooking the workshops, assistant Bill Price occupied a corner of the same space, and bulky spares, body panels and sections of cars all had to find space in there, somehow. Douggie Watts ran the workshop, Douggie Hamblin and Tommy Wellman were his able assistants, and all the mechanics (once appointed, none ever seemed to leave ...) were capable of tackling any job.

Every mechanic was expected to be able to tackle every job, so the build system at Abingdon was that when a car had to be prepared, or re-prepared, that task was allocated to one mechanic alone: he would only involve someone else if a job required more than a single man's strength or agility. A mechanic who prepared an Austin Healey 3000 might find himself working on a Mini Cooper S after that, and perhaps on a Le Mans MGB to follow ...

Because serious rally cars always had unique wiring looms and many special lights, horns and other fitting, Lucas habitually provided specialists to look after the electrical side – and, by the 1960s, so many rally cars were 'in progress' at Abingdon at any one time, that a Lucas presence was almost taken for granted.

Unlike later rally cars of the 1960s and 1970s, the Healeys lived under a different type of workshop regime, some of them enjoying long, tough, and eventful lives. Unlike later works rally cars, such as the ubiquitous Mini Cooper S, and Escort RS1600/RS1800 types (which tended to complete only two or three rallies before their entire unit-construction body shell was discarded, so that a 'new' version of an 'old' car could take shape around a new shell) they were not consumables, but were machines which were repaired, honed, and preserved at all costs.

Before preparation began, most works cars started life as complete cars which were delivered straight from the assembly lines at Abingdon (these, of course, were only a matter of yards away from the competition workshops). As Peter Browning later wrote:

"... this being the easiest way of ensuring that the mechanic [who prepared the car for its first event] at least started with all the standard parts he required. Often, finding odd standard parts to complete a car was more time-consuming that the availability of special items ..."

"The cars were totally stripped and then rally-prepared, the degree of special work and modifications obviously increasing from event to event, with the search for more power, reliability or chassis strength.

"Later, as the cars required more chassis work, rally cars were built up from bare structural frame/inner panels, to facilitate the considerable strengthening, under-frame armour-plating, double-skinning and work like the webbing of key suspension pick-up points."

According to the chassis records preserved by the BMIHT at Gaydon, it seems that all the wind-up window BJ8 types of 1964 and 1965 took shape in this way.

Personalities and star drivers
Marcus Chambers

Marcus (nicknamed 'Chub' or 'The Poor Man's Neubauer', because of his bulky build and obvious authority), already had a great background in motorsport before he joined BMC at Abingdon at the end of 1954. Having served as racing team manager at HRG in 1947 and 1948 (he had driven for the team at Le Mans in 1938 and 1939), he had served with honour in the Royal Navy during the war, and later worked on government schemes in Tanganyika and British Honduras before opening up the new Abingdon Competitions Department under John Thornley's overall control.

Starting from scratch, and after struggling to convert the MG Car Club-based works team that he inherited (the drivers were really from a 'good chaps club') into a quasi-professional organisation, he gradually turned the BMC team into a formidable rallying force. Taking good advice wherever it was offered (and most particularly from John Gott, 'the rallying policeman', who was his team captain), he never let work get entirely in the way of good living. Although he gradually built up his on-events service support operation, and went out on as many events as possible, whenever he had to choose between standing outside at a control or service point in the cold and rain, or enjoying a good meal with fine wine, the meal often came first.

It's easy to forget that Marcus had to control a big team on events which were often much more far-flung than in the modern era, and that mobile phones, satellite navigation, GPS, fax machines and computers had not been invented. His organisation – and it really was an organisation – coped by planning meticulously before the events, relying on his drivers to make many of their own decisions, and by using the telephone network of whatever country he was in: some of those telecommunications systems were still unreliable, and caused no end of heartache.

BMC team manager, Marcus Chambers, right, handing a British Saloon Car Championship wreath to Jeff Uren in 1959.

Although he was no great shakes as a competition driver, very occasionally he would enter rallies himself (though never in Healeys!), and sometimes he would go out on practice sessions, so he was usually well in touch with the progress of his cars, and of the opposition.

In the seven years that he ran the BMC team (his first autobiography was titled *Seven Year Twitch*!), he nurtured a lot of new driving talent. His biggest 'find', no question, was the remarkable Pat Moss who, with her good friend and co-driver Ann Wisdom, proved to be an ultra-fast driver – not just a good lady driver, but an ultra-competitive 'bloke', too. He also encouraged Jack Sears to be a top-line rally driver (until, that is, Jack defected to circuit racing), hired the Morley twins in 1959, and caused David Seigle-Morris to defect from the Triumph team.

Not only that, but when he decided to move on in 1961 (he took up a post in the retail motor trade), he was personally involved in choosing Stuart Turner as his successor.

Marcus returned to motorsport in 1964, running the Rootes Group's fortunes from 1964 to 1968, which included victory in the London-Sydney Marathon.

Stuart Turner

Although Turner's best-selling autobiography was titled *Twice Lucky*, few observers thought his glittering career and the way that it evolved over the years owed much to luck. Not only did he enjoy six remarkably successful years at Abingdon from 1961 to 1967, but in later years (from 1969 to 1990) he was one of the top decision-makers in Ford Motorsport, too.

After completing his National Service in the RAF, where he learned

enough Russian to be asked to take up a permanent surveillance job in Europe, Turner returned to his native Stone, in Staffordshire, and went on to train, rather un-enthusiastically, as an accountant. At the same time he took up rallying, always as a co-driver, eventually becoming the most successful in the country.

Having won the BTRDA's National Co-driver award on three occasions in the 1950s, and become the observant editor of his local motor club magazine (where he was famous for his mordant humour), he branched out even further by tackling European events. Not only did he become instantly famous in November 1960 by navigating the giant Swede, Erik Carlsson, to victory in the British RAC International Rally, but he became the first rallies editor ('Verglas') of *Motoring News* as well.

Although he always insisted that he was surprised to be offered the job of BMC Competitions Manager in 1961, he took to it with alacrity, and great skill. While he always admitted that he could not have arrived at a more favourable

Stuart Turner (in spectacles) and Timo Makinen – together they always got the best out of the Healey.

time (the Mini Cooper was new, and the Healey 3000 was still approaching maturity), he introduced an atmosphere of ruthless purpose to a still improving team.

Within a year, some of the old guard of drivers and co-drivers had been eased out, though he made sure that Pat Moss remained. Other new arrivals were Timo Makinen and Rauno Aaltonen (the original 'Flying Finns'), and Paddy Hopkirk and, eventually, deep-thinking co-drivers such as Tony Ambrose, Paul Easter and Henry Liddon. Even so, not even he could persuade Pat Moss to remain at Abingdon, for she accepted a big financial offer from Ford at the end of 1962.

It was under Turner's control that the team got down to some more serious technical development, working with Dunlop, refining its reconnaissance and pace-noting expertise, tightening up its service procedures, and becoming even more aggressive with new homologation.

By pushing every aspect of this job to the limits – not least by a careful study of homologation and event regulations – Stuart was able to optimise the performance of an already very capable team. As an experienced rallyist, not merely as a good manager, of course, he always had the confidence of his drivers, who performed better than they might have done for anyone else.

Everyone was surprised when he abruptly decided to leave BMC at the beginning of 1967, especially as he told everyone that he thought he no longer wanted to climb mountains, to stand at the side of the road getting soaked, and have to answer to his bosses for the vagaries of event organisers.

This was the moment when he handed over to Peter Browning, in as smooth a transition as could be wished for. Even so, after spending just two years with the oil company Castrol (latterly as publicity manager), he had yet another change of mind, was seduced back into the sport by Ford UK, and spent the next two decades running motorsport and public affairs at that company.

Geoff Healey

Famous for his bushy moustache, his disapproving stare at anyone with whom he clashed, and for the sheer pungency of his pipe tobacco (the pipe was ever-present), Geoffrey Healey was the most important engineering personality in the Healey Motor Company. Although Geoff's father, Donald Healey, had been the founder of the brand, and was always the inspiration behind everything that was proposed and achieved, it was Geoff and a small team of engineers who shaped and developed the cars which BMC built and sold in such big numbers from 1953 to 1970.

Much of the general layout, the strength, and the scope for improvement of the BN series can be credited to Geoff, who always made sure that the structure was rock solid, even though it was by no means as light as some of its rivals. He was never likely to design a car like the Lotuses of the period, which were often as prone to breaking as they were to finishing an event.

A chassis design engineer of great skill, capability and achievement, Geoff also had to be Healey's direct interface with Longbridge, and had to face up to the daily battles with those who he later described as the 'philistines' within BMC's management (the opinions he expressed of the later British Leyland management do not bear repeating). Even so, Geoff also forged firm friendships with people such as Eddie Maher (BMC's Coventry-based engine development chief), and between them they turned the big C-Series 6-cylinder engine into a reliable and near unbreakable competition power unit.

Although Geoff had never been a race driver himself, he sat alongside the best on occasion, especially in long-distance races like the Mille Miglia, and always seemed to know what they wanted, what they needed, and how his company could best provide it for them. Even before BMC's Abingdon Competitions Department had turned its attention to the Big Healey (initially to the 100-Six), Geoff and his colleagues at Warwick had honed the cars into very effective race machines, and the little concern also built a series of excellent, and highly-successful record-breaking machines, too.

Earlier four-cylinder cars like the 100S types were amazingly effective, even though the engines were already

obsolescent, and although they were perhaps hampered by having to use too many standard BMC components – front suspension, steering, and gearbox casings, for example – it was Geoff and his team that made it possible to hone the cars into very effective competition machines.

Often unhappy in the face of internal company politics, and facing a reluctance by BMC to carry out the innovations he proposed, Geoff could always have made the Big Healey better and faster than it was, but some of the development paths he proposed were either ignored or followed up far too late. Classic cases in point were the fact that the radius arm/increased-travel rear suspension was not adopted for years after it was first suggested, neither was the definitive, central gearchange of the later cars introduced as soon as he wished.

Even towards the end of the Big Healey's life, Geoff was still suggesting further major improvements – not least the idea of widening the entire car, and of using a 4-litre Rolls-Royce engine to transform the performance. Naturally, when BMC refused to back this, and proposed to build a badge-engineered MG MGC instead, neither he nor his father would have anything to do with it.

Once the Big Healey had died away, and evolution of the smaller Sprite/Midget (which he had also designed) was gradually taken away from him, Geoff's interest in BMC and British Leyland dissolved. Going on to conceive the Jensen-Healey of the 1970s, and to carry out much consultant engineering thereafter, he never lost touch with Austin Healeys, and particularly all the enthusiasts who loved the cars so much.

Even after Geoff and his illustrious father were taken from us, the Healey family kept its rigorous control of the brand: Margot Healey, Geoff's widow, was always an important factor in this, and may yet see the re-launch of the Healey name in the late 2000s.

Bill Price

Every business needs its unsung heroes to allow them to survive without drama. Such characters rarely reach the pinnacle of the concern, and rarely see too much limelight, but without them things simply would not work as smoothly as they should. At Abingdon, from 1960 to 1970, and when both the Healey and the Mini Coopers were at their peak, Bill Price was that man, with the bulging files, the background information, and the mass of material held

Den Green was one of the long-serving mechanics who gave so much of his career to BMC. Later, after he retired, he became a stalwart in the historic rallying scene.

from previous events to allow all planning for the future to be seamless.

When the department re-opened in 1974 after its period in suspended animation, he speedily came back from a deadly routine job in the retail motor trade, and stayed with what was now British Leyland until the last of the Triumph TR7 V8 rally cars was retired after the end of the 1980 season.

It was only after Bill produced his monumental book *The BMC/BL Competitions Department* in the 1990s that many people realised just what careful records he had been storing away for so many years. As one colleague commented at the time: "We thought he just didn't want to share a pint with us in the evenings – it now seems that he was always upstairs in his room, up-dating his diary."

Having completed his trade apprenticeship at Morris Commercial, and then his National Service, Bill joined the Competitions Department at Abingdon as a lowly office assistant. Before long he was seen to be much more capable than that, taking over new homologation duties, much of the workshop organisation, and acting as Chambers', then Turner's, stand-in team managers on many events.

Bill was one of those invaluable team players who 'oil the wheels', and fill in the gaps. It was he who would fly out to the start of events with urgently-needed spares, or fly off to the back of beyond to retrieve broken or crashed rally cars, and square the authorities or BMC dealers who had to be ignored in the rush of events. He also knew more about the shop floor staff than his bosses ever did, and was an invaluable link between them and the management hierarchy.

Meticulous as a planner, forgetting little about past events and experiences, and always ready to sort out last-minute crises, he effectively became Deputy Competitions Manager well before the title was officially conferred on him. Before, and increasingly after, he retired, he built up more 'I was there' knowledge of the famous BMC works team than any other surviving team member.

Douggie Hamblin

Nominally no more than a mechanic, but second in line to Douggie Watts on the shop floor at Abingdon, in the late 1950s and early 1960s Douggie became the development guru behind the evolution and development of the Healey 3000. According to his boss, Marcus Chambers, he always had "an excellent nose for the right mixture", and became a real expert on the Healey 3000 engines.

When the team finally decided to adopt a triple twin-choke Weber engine installation for 1962, it was Douggie's job to turn a good idea into a working, reliable, installation, which he duly did. When the time came to carry out much back-to-back testing of the installation, Hamblin was an ever-present at one of the test beds at the MG factory at Abingdon, and even on the days leading up to the 1962 Tulip Rally, where Webers were to be used for the very first time, it was Doug who took a car all the way to the Weber factory at Bologna, Italy, for final development.

It was a terrible shock for everyone to learn that Doug was killed in a road crash on his way to work as a service mechanic to the BMC team on the 1964 Monte Carlo Rally.

Pat Moss

Everyone loved Pat Moss. I have never found anyone with a word to say against her. Although she arrived in rallying with the damning tag of 'Stirling's little sister' hanging around her neck, within a couple of years she had shown just how fast, tough and capable she was going to be as a rally driver.

A map-plotting session for BMC works drivers, with (left to right) Tommy Wisdom, Ann Wisdom, Pat Moss, Willy Cave and John Sprinzel.

Within five years of joining the BMC team, she had not only become a credible lady rally driver, but had actually won the toughest of all rallies – the Liège-Sofia-Liège.

A relatively late-comer to rallying (she had spent her earlier years competing in horse jumping events, at which she was also adept), she eventually started at BMC by driving an un-competitive MG TF on the 1955 RAC Rally, though her next drive was delayed until the Monte Carlo of 1956. After graduating to Morris Minor 1000s and MG MGAs, she got her first chance to wrestle with the Big Healey (a 100-Six) on the French Alpine of 1958.

By that time there was no doubt that this slight, devastatingly pretty, and (outwardly only) insecure young lady had become an established member of the team. Although she seemed to be scatterbrained to a fault (many was the time when she left her handbag behind at a hotel, restaurant, or rally service point!), and liked to trade on the 'wide-eyed innocent' reputation which developed over

Twenty years on, two generations of famous rally drivers met for a photocall – Pat Moss (left) with Michele Mouton (the French star of the 1980s), with a 1958 works Healey and a 1980s-type Audi Quattro.

Once she came to terms with the Big Healey (she always said it frightened her, but Paddy Hopkirk said the same – and they both won events in the cars) she was often as fast as all but the two Flying Finns, and was already being measured, and compared, on a daily basis, by all her peers. Though broad-shouldered, with enough body strength to cope with these big cars, Pat was strictly the sort of active, sport-

time, she was nevertheless ferociously competitive, with great endurance and a real will to win.

Always a heavy smoker – it took its toll in later years – and seemingly hyperactive (she disliked having nothing to do, and would always be on the look-out for a diversion) Pat wanted to be busy-busy, and was apparently interested in anything which life had to offer. Her rallying partnership with Ann Wisdom (daughter of Fleet Street's motoring doyen, Tommy Wisdom) was a great success, the two not only being a professional success, but great friends, too.

Pat Moss (right) and her long-time co-driver Ann Wisdom, poring over the paperwork for a rally in the early 1960s.

loving lady who disarmed most men with her charm – yet she could also become depressed if the cars were not always in good health.

Each of her cars got nicknames (her Liège-winning Healey, URX 727, was soon known as 'Uurrxx', her long-lived Morris 1000 was 'Granny', while a singularly unlucky Healey 3000 was always known as 'The Thing'), and, of course, she had her own foibles about equipment. Like big brother Stirling, she liked her car registration numbers, and competition numbers, to have a '7' in them – but she disliked the number '13'. Accordingly it was something of a miracle that her Liège victory was achieved in a Healey carrying the event number 76 (the individual numbers of which add up to 13).

Once the Mini Cooper arrived, she was even more successful in that little car, and the workshop staff at Abingdon was almost ready to walk through fire to build her a good example of any rally car.

Having met the mountainous Swedish rally driver Erik Carlsson, the two rapidly became an item, and married in 1962. For 1963, both were courted by Ford (which offered big financial incentives that BMC could not match): Pat took up that offer, though Erik did not. Later, Pat moved on to drive for Saab and Lancia, but she was never seen as a total icon for those teams, not in the same way that she had always been at BMC.

Donald Morley

The affectionate nickname Pat Moss gave to Donald Morley – 'the Little Devil' – was incredibly apt. Outside the car, and especially when dressed in his farmer's tweeds, Donald was a small, wiry, and always courteous character, but when driving a Healey he was one of the most ferociously fast of all of BMC's works team. Although he was neither as successful or (seemingly) as comfortable

in a Mini Cooper S, he was the absolute master of the Healey, had great success in it, and made sure that he bought one of the team cars (XJB 876 – his French Alpine-winning machine) when it was finally pensioned off.

After stumbling across rallying in the 1950s when he took it up as a hobby to give him a change from his large arable farm in East Anglia, he and his non-identical twin brother Erle (the larger of the twins) used unsuitable cars (including an Austin A90 Atlantic) to succeed in British rallies. In 1959, though, he startled the world of rallying by winning the Tulip Rally in his privately-prepared Jaguar 3.4. Signed up by Marcus Chambers to join the BMC works team, he rapidly became the master of the Big Healey. Unless asked to do an event during the harvesting season

Donald Morley (left), with motorsport entrepreneur Nick Brittan, looked like the gentleman farmer he actually was, but became 'the Little Devil' when behind the wheel of a rally car.

(which they would never do), the Morleys were willing to throw the Big Healey at any challenge, on tarmac, snow and ice, or gravel.

Although never analytical of his driving talents or methods (unlike Rauno Aaltonen, who agonised over both), and certainly not brutal with his machinery (Timo Makinen, need I say more?) he was always super fast, and rarely crashed his cars. The fact that a Big Healey, when driven to the limit, could be difficult to control, seems to have escaped him, probably because he had little experience of other fast sports cars before joining BMC.

Although he and Erle often looked as if they had come to rallying from an earlier age – they usually rallied in suits, or sports jackets, with crisp shirts and ties, at a time when the thrusting young Finns were wearing racing overalls – they were always comfortable with their cars, and their tasks. As well as rallying the best and fastest Healeys of all, Donald occasionally raced them too, while he and his brother also won the GT category of the Monte Carlo

Because 1960s rallies were often riddled with regulations which favoured a 'class-improvement' index rather than outright performance, Donald was robbed of several much-deserved outright victories. Although the records show that he officially, and deservedly, won the 1961 and 1962 French Alpine rallies in Big Healeys, he also set up the best outright performance on no fewer than four Tulip rallies outright – 1962, 1963, 1964 and 1965 – and also achieved a Coupe d'Argent (Silver Cup) for being un-penalised on the tough road section of three French Alpine rallies, too. Only the most cruel bad luck (a broken rear differential in 1963) robbed him of an even more prestigious Coupe d'Or (Gold Cup) for three consecutive such runs.

The Morleys were too gentlemanly, and too committed to their farming profession, to let top-grade rallying take over their lives, and retired while they were still at their sporting peak. Prestigious offers from Porsche were refused, and they became much-admired rallying elder-statesmen instead.

Paddy Hopkirk

Behind the Irish blarney, and the readiness to share a quip and to give quotable quotes to any motoring writer, Paddy Hopkirk's genial facade hid a rally driver with steely determination, yet someone who never quite achieved as much as he thought he deserved. Amazingly enough, his most prestigious of several victories – in the 1964 Monte in a Mini Cooper S – was achieved without making any fastest stage times in the event, and in three years he only recorded one outright victory in a Big Healey (Austrian Alpine 1964). For all that, he became Fleet Street's favourite rallying personality, and kept that fame for more than thirty years after he retired.

Having begun his rallying career as a driving test specialist in Northern Ireland, Paddy then started his works career with Standard-Triumph in 1956. After falling out with Triumph team manager Ken Richardson in 1958 (that was not difficult), he left the team to join the Rootes Group team of Sunbeam Alpines and Rapiers. It was only in 1962, and with the Rapiers apparently being at their peak, that he approached Stuart Turner at BMC, proposing himself to join the team and (in his own words) "to get his hands on the Healey 3000". In a letter to Turner, at this time, he wrote: "I want to drive cars which are capable of winning rallies outright – even if I'm not!"

Even though he soon came to terms with the high-performance, but rather brutal character of the car – he took second place, overall, in the 1962 RAC behind Erik Carlsson's all-conquering Saab 96 – and finished sixth in the 1963 RAC Rally, Paddy always admitted that he never quite mastered the Healey, and that he eventually became much more relaxed when driving the works Mini Cooper S.

Even so, he went on to win the 1964 Austrian Alpine Rally (in ARX 91B, the second of the newly-prepared wind-up window BJ8s), and was impressive in Healeys on the race track. In some cases, however, Paddy was an unlucky 'nearly man' – as shown by his second place (in a BMC 1800) in the London-Sydney Marathon of 1968, and fourth in the London-Mexico World Cup Rally (in a big Triumph 2.5PI saloon).

In his very successful BMC/British Leyland years, which lasted until the entire department closed down in 1970, Paddy was a good and supportive team player, which, to those who knew him in his Triumph and Rootes Group days, came as a real surprise. The big difference, though, was that there was a huge and constantly growing sense of team spirit at Abingdon, which had never existed in other teams. Not only that, but Paddy studiously developed his good relations with the press, and became a very valuable front man for the rally team.

Rauno Aaltonen

One of the original 'Flying Finns' in the works rally team of the 1960s, Rauno became the single most successful Mini rally driver at BMC, and also the man who delivered the most prestigious Healey victory of all time – in the 1964 Spa-Sofia-Liège Marathon Rally. As an analytical and compulsive re-designer of all his rally cars, Rauno did as much as anyone to keep the Healey 3000 improving in the 1960s, and was desperately unhappy when his entry in the 1967 RAC Rally (in the last and most special of all Healeys) was aborted when the event was cancelled at the last moment.

First as a private owner in Finland, then in vast works Mercedes-Benz saloons, he caught Stuart Turner's eye on the 1961 Polish and RAC rallies, and was quickly signed up for 1962. After starting in a (privately-supported) Cooper in the 1962 Monte (where he was nearly killed in a fiery crash), he rapidly became a fully-fledged BMC works team member in mid-1962, and was the original 'Flying Finn'.

Although some of his most noteworthy victories were in Mini Cooper S types – he notched up his first outright win in the French Alpine Rally 1963 – Rauno won no fewer than nine Internationals in Minis, including five in 1965 alone, when he became European Rally Champion. Among his famous victories were the 1965 RAC Rally and the 1967 Monte – and, of course, the 1964 Spa-Sofia-Liège in a Healey 3000.

Apart from that startling Spa-Sofia-Liège success, when he virtually obliterated all his rivals, his career in Healeys was not as glittering nor as intense, and occasionally these big beasts got away from him. In particular on the Liège in 1963 when he was leading; he was lucky to come away unscathed as his co-driver, Tony Ambrose recalls that on the Passo di Vivione in Italy "Rauno slid the car just a bit wide, over-corrected, and clouted a rock face. Rauno again over-corrected, the Healey gave a vicious swerve, hit the rocks again, and then spun away across the road, and crashed head-first through the railings. Why we never went right over the edge I will never know ... I will never forget that when I opened my door to step out there was nothing but fresh air, and the car was balanced on the brink ..." Perhaps it was appropriate that this particular works Healey – 77 ARX – was never used again!

Even so, Rauno was super smooth as a driver, and was only rarely a crasher. He was always the team's great thinker, the one with the most good ideas, and had a tendency to sketch those ideas on the back of envelopes, service schedules, and even on restaurant tablecloths. Some found his compulsion to fiddle with specifications rather irritating, but others found his mild, good mannered, character very appealing, and when super-fast times were needed, no-one delivered more consistently than Rauno.

When the Healey's front-line life as a rally car came to an end, Rauno was still reaching his personal peak, and he went on to achieve great things for BMC driving Mini Cooper Ss. In 1968, after the formation of British Leyland, Rauno didn't really leave the team, rather the team left him. When Lord Stokes demanded big changes at Abingdon, Rauno's (and Timo Makinen's) contracts were torn up. Having dabbled with Lancia and, in later years, with Nissan, Rauno became a much sought-after ambassador for European manufacturers like BMW. To his great sorrow, he never won the Safari, though he finished second on four occasions.

Unlike other stars of the 1960s, Rauno never got involved in the growing and glamorous world of historic rallying, preferring to make his living as a teacher and a representative of various manufacturers. With BMW, he once demonstrated the crash test capability of a restraint system by taking the place of the 'dummy': Rauno, naturally, had done all his research and knew it was safe.

Timo Makinen

From the time he first saw him to this day, when questioned

Many years after the Healey had been retired, Timo Makinen (left) and co-driver Mike Wood were reunited with this privately-owned car in the historic section of the Manx Rally.

about his illustrious past, BMC rally team boss Stuart Turner has no doubts, that Timo (the second of the 'Flying Finns') was the fastest rally driver in the world. For more than a decade – 1962 until the mid-1970s – Timo probably started every rally as the favourite, and led most of them. Although he rarely crashed, he was hard on his cars, expecting his team to build machinery that would withstand his methods.

Originally something of a wild-man in his native Finland

Timo Makinen and 67 ARX in full cry, in the 1989 Pirelli Classic Marathon. The Healey was already 27 years old when this picture was taken, but it doesn't show!

(among his exploits was racing a Jaguar D-Type on ice, on spiked tyres!), Timo got a trial in the BMC works team after the Finnish importer called Stuart Turner to plead his case. Within a year he had mastered Mini Coopers and Austin Healey 3000s, and no-one else could match him.

Although Timo never actually won an event in a Healey 3000, he was certainly the bravest, the fastest and probably the most spectacular behind the wheel of the big red sports cars. It was his amazing class and category performances in Healeys which endeared him to so many fans – a class win in the wintriest of all the Monte Carlo rallies, with Christabel Carlisle alongside him in 1963, and second overall in back-to-back RAC rallies, 1964 and 1965 being just two such bravura displays.

Timo Makinen was probably the fastest driver ever to grapple with a Big Healey – yet never won a major event in one.

The Old Firm reunited – Timo Makinen and Paul Easter, with the nicely-maintained 67 ARX, at the finish of the 1989 Pirelli Classic Marathon in Cortina, Italy.

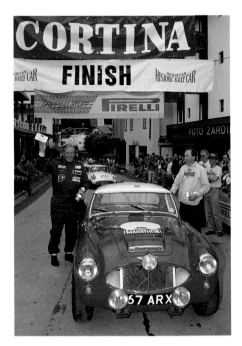

Like other BMC team members of the day, Timo won many major internationals in Mini Cooper Ss, while in a later sporting life he also won three RAC rallies in Ford Escorts. He seemed to lead almost every rally he ever started, but his machinery often let him down. Observers reckon that his 1965 Monte victory (in a Mini) was the best rally drive of all time, but others remember that 1965 RAC Rally in a Healey (EJB 806C, brand new for the occasion), where he was demonstrably the fastest of all on snow, ice, deep mud, and sometimes hard gravel, was only denied victory by Rauno Aaltonen's Mini Cooper S, which could get more grip, more often.

In a word, as a rally driver Timo was spectacular and, let us be honest, almost impossible to control by his co-drivers. When the situation demanded it (and at other times, too, when he felt like it), Timo was a more flamboyant driver than any of his team mates, more sideways, more energetic, and behind the wheel was demonstrably putting more effort into his driving than they were. A co-driver had to be brave to control such a massive personality, and it was the mild-mannered Paul Easter who managed this best of all.

When Timo and his car were on song, no-one – not even Rauno Aaltonen, certainly not Paddy Hopkirk – could match his pace in similar machines. To see Timo in full flow – particularly from the terrifying vantage point of the passenger seat – was an awe-inspiring experience.

Certainly he drove his cars harder than anyone else of the period, expecting them to put up with his brutal methods, and to withstand assault from the rough special stage tracks. Big Healeys were better than Minis at putting up with this, though he was not often given the chance to prove that.

As with Rauno Aaltonen, Timo left the BMC team in 1968 after Lord Stokes culled the department. Since both the Healey and the Mini were over their peak, he was, in any case, falling out with the team, and despised the BMC 1800 'Landcrabs' which were replacing them.

Later, ex-BMC team boss Stuart Turner persuaded him to join the Ford team in 1970, and he then enjoyed seven seasons at Boreham. Three RAC Rally wins were a highlight of this period, as were other individual highlights. Management did not enjoy his meddling with specifications, though, and he was released at the end of 1976.

Competition story

It wasn't until 1958 that a major change of strategy came, very tentatively, to Abingdon, when Marcus Chambers and his team turned their attention to the Big Healey at last. Although the works team begun that season with the same old rag-bag of uncompetitive BMC models, there was at least the prospect of the more powerful (but unproven) MGA Twin-Cam becoming available in mid-season (its launch was forecast for the first half of the year, but like all such BMC programmes, it slipped by months ...), a car which promised to have a better power/weight ratio than any previous BMC rally car.

In the meantime, however, Tommy Wisdom, who was not only a long-time friend of Donald Healey, but also an experienced competition driver and a very powerful and influential national newspaper motoring journalist, had been nagging at BMC's managing director, George Harriman, for some time, telling him that, in his opinion, the latest 100-Six model could be successful in rallying. Accordingly, for the Sestriere Rally, an Italian event to be held in February 1957, Harriman agreed to let him use a car which the Warwick racing department (not the works rally team) would prepare.

1957

The very first, the original works Big Healey rally car, therefore, was UOC 741, a BN4 which had already had a varied career, which would become even more complex in the future. Carrying a very early BN4 chassis number, in the summer of 1956 this car had started life as one of the first six-cylinder Austin Healeys to be assembled on the production line at Longbridge, and became an open-top publicity machine. At the time, it seems, it was about to be pensioned off from the press fleet, and unless

Wisdom was to be provided with a new car (which Harriman was not inclined to approve, on the grounds of cost), it was effectively the only car that could be spared.

It now sounds pathetic to relate, but as there was virtually no Big Healey rallying or preparation expertise on record in 1957, and absolutely none at all at Warwick, preparation for the Sestriere, to a hard-top specification, was laid down by Tommy Wisdom himself. Although this might sound outlandish, and amateurish in the extreme, it was not, for Tommy had been driving all manner of race and rally cars since the 1930s; he knew what he wanted, and what he might be comfortable with.

Among the changes made to this car were larger (Armstrong DAS10) lever arm rear dampers to improve control of the rear axle movement, and the hard-top featured a then fashionable swivelling spot lamp, which had a handle inside the cabin for use by the co-driver. The engine, though, was left standard, which meant that, with little more than 100bhp, it was not likely to be a potential winner.

Although there was no success for the Wisdom family in the Sestriere (Tommy took his daughter, Ann, with him, who was already in the BMC works team as Pat Moss' co-driver), Tommy apparently put in a very thoughtful and valuable report, suggesting what might be done to make a promising car better. Incidentally, BMC sent three works cars to the same Sestriere event (a Morris Minor 1000, an MG Magnette and an Austin A105!), but took no interest in what Tommy was doing.

The self-same car, UOC 741, was suitably re-prepared (with a prototype BN6 engine, whose much better cylinder head made it a more formidable proposition), and finished

For the 1958 Monte Carlo Rally, UOC 741 had this fascia style, complete with clocks ahead of the co-driver's seat, and a Halda speed pilot on the transmission tunnel.

honourably in the 1957 Mille Miglia. On this, the last-ever of those 1000 mile open road races in Italy, Tommy Wisdom and Cecil Winby (who worked for the Brico pistons company in Coventry) took 37th place out of a field of 365 cars. Incidentally, BMC race cars still looked relatively standard in those days, for on the Mille Miglia the 100-Six carried its front and rear bumpers.

1958

Even so, it would still be some time before the works Competitions Department took much interest in this particular car or model, for it was still being maintained at Warwick. However, its next appearance was in the 1958 Monte Carlo Rally, when Tommy Wisdom and Cyril Smith borrowed it yet again. In an event which has now gone down in history

Ready for the 1958 Monte Carlo Rally is the 100-Six UOC 741, not yet an official works rally car – though it would eventually join the Abingdon fleet.

as being the worst-weather Monte of all time, UOC 741 was eventually eliminated in the blizzard. However, it must have made something of an impression on Marcus Chambers at the time for, according to Geoffrey Healey:

"Marcus Chambers, then heading BMC competition, had been persevering with the more mundane BMC vehicles in competition, and quickly saw the potential of the car. He rang me and persuaded me to lend him the car for some rallies. We were also able to let him have drawings and specifications of all the special parts and equipment used. Syd Enever [MG's chief designer] redesigned the rear spring to reduce the stress under load and produced the legendary 14-leaf rear spring that was to contribute so much to the success of the 6-cylinders. With the departure of UOC 741 to Abingdon [which presumably means that the 'loan' to Marcus Chambers soon turned into a permanent arrangement] our involvement in rallies was greatly reduced."

At this point, it is important to stress that it was Geoff Healey's team at Warwick which had already developed the four-wheel disc brake installation which was to make so much difference to the capability of these cars, and which featured on all 100-Six and 3000s rallied from 1958 on.

Although Group 3 homologation normally made no provision for disc brakes to be approved as an alternative to drums (or front-disc/rear-drum on the 3000), the regulations

Jack Sears – 'Gentleman Jack' to all who knew him – was one of the fastest and most capable of those who ever drove a Big Healey.

Jack Sears and Peter Garnier drove UOC 741 on the 1958 Tulip Rally, but the car had to retire with a broken engine distributor drive.

stated that if such a kit had been put on sale, and sufficient numbers sold, then approval would follow. But just how many four-wheel disc kits were sold? "Enough," BMC staff would say with wide eyes and an innocent expression – and both the RAC and FIA inspectors believed them. This was just the first of many innovations which gradually turned the basic car into a formidable special competition car.

For BMC at Abingdon, however, the era of the works Healeys had only just begun. For the next eight years these machines were the most charismatic of the fleet of cars, and

All works Austin Healey 100-Six and 3000 types had this type of curvaceous lift-off hard-top – though such optional fittings seemed to be surprisingly rare on road cars.

they were still being improved in 1965 when their rallying career was finally cut off. UOC 741's first Abingdon-prepared appearance was in the 1958 RAC Rally, where racing driver Jack Sears and Peter Garnier (who was sports editor of *Autocar*) struggled without success against very wintry conditions. This was an event which proved to be a battle for sporting survival, and to visit all the controls (which the Healey did not) was essential to success. To take fifth in class was a disappointment for this highly dedicated crew.

In the meantime, Abingdon was learning rapidly about the Big Healey, and its rugged structure. Only weeks after the RAC Rally, the same car/crew combination performed splendidly on the hillclimbs and speed tests of the Tulip Rally before the fuel pump and the distributor drive both failed, forcing the car to retire. As Jack Sears later recalled:

"I remember how impressed I was with ... the tremendous pulling power of the engine. The factory was sufficiently encouraged to run this car

Nancy Mitchell about to start the 1958 French Alpine Rally from the quayside in Marseilles, with Bill Shepherd's PMO 202 (seventh overall) ready to follow her over the ramp.

again for Peter and me in the 1958 Tulip Rally. Although the car retired towards the end with a broken distributor when we were lying second in class [behind a Mercedes-Benz 300SL, so no shame in that!] and tenth overall, we managed to achieve some very fast times on the special stage hillclimbs. This convinced BMC that the car had class-winning potential, and that they should continue development and embark on a full programme of events ..."

How many more times in the years to come would a C-Series engine suffer from distributor problems? Was there some kind of vibration problem which was never solved?

For the first full team effort – the French Alpine Rally of 1958 – BMC entered no fewer than five 100-Six BN6 models. No other makes or models of works BMC cars were prepared, but even so, there was a tremendous rush even to get them to the start line, as Marcus Chambers later explained: "We had at one time hoped to enter five Twin-Cam MGAs but for a number of reasons this was not possible [in the event, the launch of the Twin-Cam was delayed, the car only being unveiled the week after the Alpine Rally took place] and at the last minute we decided to enter the same number of Austin Healey 100-Sixes.

"Owing to the change in our plans,

Seen here on the slopes of Mont Ventoux, Nancy Mitchell drove TON 792 on the Alpine Rally of 1958, and finished 12th overall.

Nancy Mitchell and Anne Hall pose with a very smart TON 792, before the start of the 1958 Liège-Rome-Liège ...

... but after four days and nights, neither they, nor the car, were as smart.

On its second event in two months, Joan Johns' 100-Six tackles the Liège-Rome-Liège marathon.

Safety – what safety?

Times and standards have changed dramatically in the four decades since the Healey was seen as the formidable last word in rally cars. Even so, it is a sobering thought that, in those days, rally cars did not have these:

Safety roll cages – the technology was known in the USA, but frowned upon by British scrutineers.

Plumbed-in fire extinguishing systems – these had not yet been made available for private cars. Rally cars tended to carry small extinguishers clipped into the spares/tool-carrying space.

Foam-filled fuel tanks – these were not even available in the 1960s.

Run-flat tyres with mousse – not yet invented.

Driver-to-navigator intercoms – the technology was available, via the RAF, but was costly, and not very efficient.

Full-harness safety belts – most rally crews used three-point belts; some diehards still refused to wear them.

Flame-proof overalls – the technology was unknown, and padded suits were not yet invented. Racing overalls kept one clean, but that was about all, and any so-called fire-proofing leached out when they were washed. (The Morley twins, incidentally, habitually drove Healeys in tweed suits, or in sports jackets and flannels ...)

Artificial stimulants – in the early 1960s, not only were Benzedrine/Dexedrine 'pep pills' still legal, but could be (and were) available from one's doctor. For events like Spa-Sofia-Liège, where there was no more than one official stop of one hour in a 96-hour marathon, some form of 'upper' was almost essential to keep going ...

Safety steering columns – have you ever studied the steering column layout of a 100-Six or 3000? The column was one straight and stiff tube, connecting the steering box ahead of the line of the front wheels, with the steering wheel ahead of the driver's chest. Amazingly, no-one ever seems to have had a serious injury related to this layout.

there was little time to carry out much testing or to do any of our own development work, although we had been lent the duo-tone green demonstrator [UOC 741] from the Donald Healey Motor Company. This car had most of the chassis modifications which had been developed by Geoffrey Healey and was fitted with Dunlop disc brakes on all four wheels. We added the alternative [SU] twin-carburettor equipment, larger fuel tanks and twin spare wheels.

"As we only had three cars of our own in addition to the Healey Company's demonstrator, we had to borrow another demonstrator from the Austin Motor Company. This car was red and black, and was normally used by the Vice Chairman, Mr George Harriman. He very sportingly released it for this event and we allotted it to Nancy Mitchell. The three other cars were bright red, a colour which I consider lucky and which has since come to be regarded as the BMC team colour. These were captained by Jack Sears, Pat Moss and Bill Shepherd. The green car naturally went to John Gott, who had a preference for this colour."

Except for the fact that this was the very first time Pat Moss had driven a Big Healey (up to then she was more used to driving far less powerful Morris Minor 1000s), this was almost the usual full-strength BMC team. The experienced hands, including top policeman John Gott, and race driver Jack Sears, could not wait to get their hands on a car which promised to be powerful enough to deal with the big hills, tight timing, and sinuous roads of this classic rally.

Distinguished Healey historian Peter Browning puts the reason for choosing Big Healeys down to this: "To celebrate the occasion of 100-Six production being moved from Longbridge to Abingdon alongside the current MG range ..." – which is romantic enough, but surely not correct, as that assembly move had taken place in the autumn of 1957, at least nine months earlier.

In fact, these cars were still only at the beginning of their evolution, and although they put up a brave show, which was vividly captured on film by the Shell Film Unit, their first appearance was not a great success.

Not only did they strike the usual (and frankly, expected) teething troubles of a newly-developed competition car (which included John Gott's car losing a wheel, complete with hub, and Pat Moss' suffering clutch slip after a 'helpful' journalist had tied up an engine breather pipe at a service halt, thus causing oil to be diverted to the wrong places), but Jack Sears' car suffered accidental damage following a brush with another competitor on the Croce Domini pass in the Italian Dolomites.

Even so, Bill Shepherd performed well to win a Coupe des Alpes with an unpenalised run, and took seventh overall, while Pat Moss and Nancy Mitchell finished first and second in the well-publicised Ladies Award category. It wasn't quite the fairy-tale start that everyone had wanted, for this was the event in which Ken Richardson's works Triumph TR3As appeared for the first time with a 2.2-litre engine, this being just enough to win the class. Even so, and as far as I can see, this was the first and only time that a TR3A beat a Big Healey in a straight fight.

The promise of the new cars was there, for sure, as the early-event pace of Jack Sears' car (PMO 203), and Bill Shepherd's Coupe-winning performance (in PMO 202) had confirmed. With more power – naturally the drivers all wanted more power! – and with ever-improving reliability, these could become formidable fighting machines. If only we had known, the true Big Healey era – an eight-year programme – had now begun.

Following the encouraging Alpine Rally performance, Abingdon's mechanics hastily repaired four of the cars to compete in the Liège-Rome-Liège event. Because Abingdon was still – and always would be – short of fully-prepared rally cars which could be spared for practice and reconnaissance tasks, only one of the ex-Alpine Rally machines (the original car, UOC 741) could be spared for mundane duties.

Pat Moss and Nancy Mitchell used their ex-Alpine Rally cars, but Gerry Burgess took over from Bill Shepherd in PMO 202, while Joan Johns drove PMO 203 instead of John Gott (who was allocated a new MGA Twin-Cam Coupé for the occasion). Three of the big Healeys – a 'man's car' if ever we saw one – would therefore be driven by ladies on this, the most gruelling of events.

Even by 1958, 'the Liège' had built up a fearsome reputation. Not only were its competitors faced with the prospect of driving, and staying awake except for naps in the moving car, for up to four days and nights, but this event featured the highest target average speeds of all European events, and ventured deep into Yugoslavia, where summer temperatures were high, the roads were rough, the loose stones and rocks were hard and destructive, and the dust seemed to get everywhere. A Big Healey rally car was never airtight or watertight at the best of times, so an event like the Liège was sure to be tough on car and crew.

As Pat Moss later said: "It was like driving over an enormous washboard with a loose gravel surface, clouds of dust, mountains with twisty roads, and almost tropical heat ... Yugoslavia always shatters hopes and cars ... The Healey is a low car with not much ground clearance, and the under-part had a terrible bashing on the rough. But they were strong, those Healeys, built like tanks, and nothing broke. It is incredible how tough they are, when they look so sporty ... [however] The engine was like a furnace, and more heat came backwards into the car. The exhaust pipe was under the co-driver's seat so there was heat burning upwards as well ..."

Marcus Chambers recognised all this, but was convinced that, of all the cars available to him in the BMC fleet (and there seemed to be any number of cars at Abingdon in those days) he had found the ideal. As he commented when he wrote his autobiography *Seven Year Twitch* (which was later expanded and re-published as *Works Wonders*): "In 1958, the Austin Healey 100-Six seemed the right wear for the Liège. We had long felt that we needed a car with long, hairy, legs to stride over the mountains and great lungs with which to rush up the hills; this seemed to be it."

And so it was. In spite of the conditions, it was only Joan Johns' PMO 203 which did not make it to the finish, this car having suffered steering damage after leaving the road close to the Italian border near Tarvisio. Even that could be repaired by the BMC service crews – and was – so that Joan rejoined the support convoy as potential 'spares on the hoof', and made it back to Belgium with the rest of the team.

Three of the four cars (two driven by ladies) finished this car-breaker, BMC won the Manufacturers' Team Prize with its sturdy Healeys, and the amazing Pat Moss, who really didn't look big enough or strong enough to wrestle with a Big Healey (and it was only her second rally in one of those cars), finished fourth overall. By doing so, incidentally, Pat broke every team order that Marcus Chambers handed out:

'She went better and better as the rally ran on ... I kept telling her to take it easy, and on arriving in England again. Later, I received a press photograph of the girls being welcomed at Spa; it was inscribed, 'To Sir, who said "Slower", from "Faster and Faster"'

From that moment, the Big Healey became BMC's fastest and most popular works rally car – popular with the drivers, who liked its potential, popular with the BMC

mechanics, who knew that it would always be worth sweating to improve it, and popular with the spectators because it had such charisma. Whenever and wherever a Big Healey stopped at a control or a service point – and particularly if that gruff six-cylinder engine was revved up, it would attract a ring of admirers.

Steady development would make them faster, stronger, and ever more competitive – and because a great deal of thought always went into homologating the best possible engine, transmission and chassis options, this effectively made the Big Healey the very first of the 'homologation specials'. Other manufacturers (like Rootes with its Sunbeam Rapiers) tried to match them, but did not start from the same promising base, while manufacturers like Triumph and Porsche eventually squandered the advantage of starting with promising cars, but not improving them anything like as much.

Not that it means that a Big Healey was easy to drive on the limit, particularly on low-grip surfaces such as gravel or snow and ice. To this day, the ever-modest Pat Moss insists that she was always frightened of the cars, not only when they were new to her, but in later years when a Big Healey had become very fast indeed, and that "if one started sliding, and you didn't catch it after two snakes, it was goodbye and goodnight!" Peter Riley used a cricketing term to describe the chassis and the traction: "If you gave it a footful off the line, or out of a tight corner, it would take off – straight towards mid-off!" Even Paddy Hopkirk, who joined BMC from Rootes in 1962, specifically to get his hands on the Big Healey, now says that he never mastered it, and that he was eventually happy to specialise in Mini Coopers instead.

Not that any aspiring hero ever turned down a chance to be a star. To my knowledge, every BMC team member wanted to drive a Big Healey if he or she ever got the chance, and until 1965 there was always a queue to compete in them. They were, after all, ultra-competitive – and everyone loves a winner. Once the 3000s had taken over from the 100-Sixes in mid-1959, they were rarely headed in their class or category (it needed a phenomenally fast car like a four-cam-engined Porsche Carrera, or early 911, or even

Jack Sears in full flight on the Zandvoort circuit, on his way to a fine class win in the 1959 Tulip Rally. PMO 203 was originally a 100-Six that was eventually converted to 3000 specification.

a Mercedes-Benz 300SL, to do that), and by the time a series of homologation moves had been made in 1960, they were always likely to win any high-speed rally where the classification handicaps, or maybe the appalling road surfaces, were not against them.

1959

Although two of the 1958 cars were sold off at the end of the season, the most recently-developed PMO cars (PMO 201, PMO 202 and PMO 203) were all rebuilt after the 1958 Liège,

and made ready for 1959. There was, however, no rush to get them ready, for no-one seemed interested in sending very powerful cars to compete in the Monte Carlo and Sestriere rallies early in the season. Monte Carlo, in fact, saw a typical marketing-inspired entry of six cars, of four different models!

Bystanders must have wondered why there was so little emphasis on the Big Healey in the first months of 1959, for they could not have known that a new model – the original 3000 – was on the way, and would make the works team's prospects even more formidable.

This extremely rare colour shot shows two of the works 3000s – Bill Shepherd's SMO 744, and John Gott's SMO 745 (5th in the GT category) – on the 1959 French Alpine Rally.

Two of the team's 3000s in a brief moment of rest, before the difficult sections of the 1959 Liège-Sofia-Liège began. The car carrying competition number 81 was driven by Jack Sears and Peter Garnier.

Two of the works 3000s on the Aintree circuit test of the 1959 RAC Rally – Jack Sears driving SMO 746, Donald Morley in SMO 745. Morley finished fourth overall, having fought his way around snow-blocked roads in the Scottish hills.

The Healey's first works appearance in 1959 was in the Tulip Rally – which was the usual mixture of speed hillclimbs, circuit tests, and a difficult-to-overcome performance handicap imposed by the Dutch organisers. Driving PMO 203, Jack Sears and Peter Garnier took a fine eighth place in the 1959 Tulip Rally, where they also won their capacity class, though Pat Moss' sister car (PMO 202) was eliminated in a severe accident on a wet road: it was very badly damaged, and was not used again by the works team.

As expected, Jack set a series of splendid times throughout, defeating well-driven Ferrari 250GTs, Aston-Martin DB2/4s and Mercedes-Benz 300SLs in his capacity class. Although he set fastest times, outright, on more than one test (including that at the Zandvoort race circuit), the handicapping system meant that he could never challenge for outright victory.

Incidentally, this was the event in which two modest, but talented and determined, farming twins from East Anglia – Donald and Erle Morley – astonished everyone by keeping a clean sheet in their privately-owned Jaguar 3.4-litre saloon, and by winning the event outright. Marcus Chambers was so impressed by that performance they had made sure that the Morleys soon joined the works team at BMC. As we now know, in future years they would go on to be the most consistently successful of all crews in Austin Healey 3000s.

Only one other works 100-Six ever started a rally in 1959 – PMO 201, on the Greek Acropolis Rally, driven by Pat Moss – but it was a downbeat way to end a career, for this car crashed with co-driver Ann Wisdom at the wheel. As Pat later admitted, she had to make a phone call saying: "Marcus, we've done it again ..."

The arrival of the 3000

As far as rallying was concerned, the team's prospects were transformed in mid-summer 1959 when the larger-engined, front-disc-braked, 3000 appeared, and was quickly homologated. Because road car assembly had begun at Abingdon several weeks before the 3000 was officially announced, many cars had already been built and shipped to the USA. Group 3 sporting homologation was achieved at once, which meant that Abingdon could start to use 3000s immediately – in fact, on the French Alpine Rally.

The records show that Abingdon built up three brand-new cars – SMO 744, SMO 745 and SMO 746 for this event – and that one of the old 100-Six types (PMO 203) was converted to a 3000, and used later in the season. As far as the drivers were concerned, the cars they were to drive were much the same as before – same structure, same transmission, and same four-wheel-disc brake set up – but they now had torquey 2912cc engines instead of 2639cc. Although that was only a ten per cent enlargement in engine capacity, it delivered the same amount of extra torque, and made them even more competitive than before.

Even so, it was not until the end of the year that the new car took the results which it truly deserved. Although John Gott finished fifth in category in the French Alpine, the other two cars both retired. It was the same catalogue of disasters on the Liège-Rome-Liège which followed, where all four of the current 3000 'fleet' started the event but three of them retired – two because they ran out of time on an event with almost insanely high target average speeds. Somehow, though, Peter Riley kept going, and won his capacity class.

The tide then turned, for although BMC sent only a single Big Healey (SMO 746) on the German Rally in October, for Pat Moss to drive, and with limited service support, she set many fastest times during the event and, if justice had been done, would have earned victory. Unhappily, the organisers were imposing a class improvement handicap (the car which did best relative to its other class competitors automatically finished higher), which meant that Pat could only finish second overall. [The win, incidentally, went to Erik Carlsson in his astonishing little Saab 96. It was not long before Erik and Pat became close – and they would marry in 1962, though the sporting rivalry between them never ceased.]

Finally, in November, BMC entered almost every rally car that it could find in the 'home' international, the RAC – which meant that eight cars turned up, of which three cars

Tulip Rally 1960, with two Healeys in formation on a road section – Donald Morley followed by Pat Moss.

were 3000s, all being the latest SMO cars.

If the rally had gone according to the organisers' plans, it would have presented a tough open-road and navigational challenge, with circuit tests and special tests to help provide a result, As it happened, there was heavy snow in the Scottish mountains, north of the Braemar time control, about which the organisers knew in advance, though they do not seem to have passed on this information to the competitors.

This meant that many cars were marooned in drifts for hours on the mountain roads, and automatically put out of the running. Running at the head of the field, Johnny Williamson never stood a chance of getting through, though team mates Donald Morley and Jack Sears both turned back and flew round the blockage by extra-mileage main roads. Amazingly, the Morley twins (on their very first works drive in a Healey) reached Braemar, though 44 minutes late, and were eventually classified fourth overall, winning their class, though Jack Sears could not get there inside the 60-minute lateness

Pat Moss/Ann Wisdom drove this 3000 – URX 727 – into a fine second place in the 1960 French Alpine Rally – but it would perform even better on the Liège that followed.

URX 727, in which Pat Moss and Ann Wisdom won the 1960 Liège-Rome-Liège, is arguably the most famous Big Healey of all time. Lovingly preserved by later owners, it looks equally as good today, as it did when new.

Pat Moss and Ann Wisdom astonished the entire rallying establishment by winning the 1960 Liège-Rome-Liège marathon in URX 727, which proved supreme in the mountains, and on the rough roads of the Balkans.

John Gott's 3000 (SMO 746) was one of three works cars which performed so well in the Liège-Rome-Liège of 1960.

Peter Riley in the oldest of all 3000s – SJB 471 – on the Stelvio Pass in the Liège-Rome-Liège of 1960.

period, and dropped to 17th, and second in class. It was a frustrating end to a promising season.

1960

The real breakthrough for the Healey came in 1960. Although most of the BMC drivers were ageing, and becoming less competitive with the young heroes who were

flooding into motorsport, the still-youthful Pat Moss seemed to be getting faster, and more determined, every season.

For Pat, though, the year started badly, when her old car (SMO 746, tricked up to look like SMO 745 after a pre-rally accident to the earlier machine!) suffered a bad accident at the Solitude race circuit on the Lyon-Charbonnieres rally. Pat was lucky to escape with no more than a nose bleed, for a railway sleeper from a circuit banking reinforcement penetrated the cockpit, missing her by inches: amazingly, that car would eventually be rebuilt around a new shell/structure and major components.

The SMO cars were unlucky for almost everyone, though Pat then took seventh on the Geneva Rally in SMO 745. Using SMO 744 (she nicknamed it 'The Thing' – I guess because she didn't like it!) – she then retired from the Circuit of Ireland, with transmission failure.

The tide then turned for BMC and the Healey – especially for Pat Moss and a brand-new car, URX 727. First of all, Pat took 'Uurrxx', as she always called it, to eighth in the Tulip Rally, beating the Morley twins in a sister car (and that, on the Tulip, was a rare occasion).

Then came the French Alpine, which was an ideal test for the latest Big Healey, where no fewer than four works cars took the start. It was on this event that Pat astonished everyone (including herself for, as noted, she always said she was frightened of the Healey's habits!) by taking second place overall, being only beaten by an extremely special Zagato-bodied Alfa Romeo Giulietta SZ, with no-one else close. In a very good showing by BMC, John Gott's car was eighth (second in class) and the Morleys took third in the same class.

Now everyone was taking notice, not only because the Healey (now in homologated triple-SU-carburettor form) was looking very purposeful, but because Pat had thoroughly shrugged

off her 'Stirling's little sister' tag. As *Autocar*'s rally report concluded: "In particular, the stirring performance of Pat Moss and Ann Wisdom will be remembered with pride whenever British achievements in Continental rallies are discussed."

After Pat's remarkable performance in the Alpine, everyone was expecting great things on the Liège. This time Marcus Chambers' memory was that "the Healey 3000s were beautifully prepared and in a slightly better form than when they had been so successful in the Alpine Rally only two months before [at this point they were probably running with about 160-180bhp/2912cc engines]."

"On returning to England we had gone over the weak points of the cars and had come to the conclusion that we were now getting more power than the gearboxes could

Donald Morley, as ever wearing his sports jacket and hat, about to re-start his Healey from the overnight halt in Scotland on the 1960 RAC Rally. Donald and his twin-brother Erle took third place overall.

stand ... I therefore approached Charles Griffin, the Chief Engineer of BMC, with our problem, and he asked for the loan of one of the Alpine cars. I think everyone was pleasantly surprised with the experience and, as a result, there was an amused twinkle in Charles' eyes when I asked for better gearboxes ... To tip the scales a little in our favour, I wrote a memo to Charles, with a copy to John Thornley, in which I said we would win the Liège if we had the right gear ratios."

Marcus had become adept at this type of lobbying. At this time, for instance, Charles Griffin was running the development programme for cars like the still-secret front-wheel drive BMC 1100, which was technically elegant but not a high performer, so persuading him to drive a noisy, hairy-chested, out-and-out works rally car must have been a real experience for him.

As a result, Marcus got his gears, Pat Moss elected to run with a very low rear axle ratio (the gear set, reputedly, coming from that of an Austin taxicab!), and a fairy-tale result was achieved. The story of that amazing Liège-Rome-Liège marathon has been told many times. Here I need only summarise: BMC entered four works 3000s for the four-day/four-night event, with no overnight rest halts of any type. This started in Belgium, struck deep into Yugoslavia, travelled through Northern Italy, and into the French Alps, before returning to Belgium. It was not only a car breaker, but one with incredibly tight time schedules, and many crews fell out due to a mixture of exhaustion, car problems, and the sheer difficulty of keeping up with the clock.

Even so, only one Healey was forced out (Peter Riley's engine let go, after a sticking throttle made it over-rev on an early section). John Gott's car finished tenth, new recruit David Seigle-Morris (who had defected from the failing Triumph team) finished fifth, while the amazing girls – Pat Moss and Ann Wisdom – won the event outright.

Not only was this the first outright win ever achieved by a 3000, but it was recorded on the toughest of all Internationals – and it was the first time that an all-female crew had won a major European rally. Add to this the fact that BMC won the team prize, and I can understand why

Marcus Chambers later wrote that this was the "highlight of my career as a Competition Manager ..."

All this, mind you, followed a worrying time in mid-event when the winning car suffered a gearbox problem after the drain plug fell out, when a new oil seal was needed, and had to be fitted in a wayside garage immediately before the Col d'Allos! Nor was this a special seal, but one which was cobbled up from supplies for French cars which just happened to be available on the premises.

After this, a fine drive by the Morley twins' into third place in the RAC Rally (behind Carlsson's winning Saab 96, and John Sprinzel's Sebring Sprite) was almost an anti-climax, and there was now no doubt that the Healey was capable of winning any event where it could get enough traction.

1961

By comparison with 1960, where the Healey had set new standards for itself, most of the 1961 season was also an anti-climax for the team. This was a season in which the Big Healeys often struggled to match Hans-Joachim Walter's Porsche 356 Carrera for pace, and to beat various performance-negating handicaps. Although this car was nominally 'private' Walter, the German scrap metal dealer, was well-connected at the Porsche factory in Stuttgart, and seemed to get his car re-prepared, and modernised, better and faster than was otherwise to be expected.

Although BMC built up no fewer than five brand-

Opposite top: This was the short-lived 3000 MkII engine/ gearbox of 1961, showing the three SU carburettors and the earlier-type transmission, complete with direct-action change-speed lever, and optional overdrive ...

Opposite bottom: ... while this is one of the very-last pre-Weber carb works engines, with three 2.0in SU carbs, the homologated six-branch exhaust manifold, and the final type of transmission, complete with remote-control gearchange mechanism and a new gearbox casing.

Pat Moss/Ann Wisdom in XJB 877, brand-new for the occasion, on the Tulip Rally of 1961, where they won their class, and, of course, the Ladies' award.

Springtime in France on the 1961 Tulip Rally, with Pat Moss (who won her class in XJB 877) leading Donald Morley through a peaceful French village on the way to another speed hillclimb.

new works cars for the season – the XJB models – there were no major Healey entries before the Tulip Rally in May. Once again this was an event dominated by speed tests, but hampered by a class-performance-improvement marking system. When I point out that this event was eventually won by a privately-entered Triumph Herald after the works Herald retired to tip the 'improvement' balance of marking, the point is surely made.

The fact that the two Healeys were fastest of all on most tests did not help, especially as neither gave way to the other to try to fudge the marking – and because there was a very purposefully-driven Mercedes-Benz 300SL close behind in the same class. In the end, BMC had to be satisfied with a class win, and (along with Tom Gold and his Sprite) the manufacturers' team prize.

After Peter Riley had put up a fine show in the Acropolis Rally (third overall in the new XJB 871, and the winner of the GT category), it was time to concentrate on the French Alpine Rally, where BMC entered no fewer

This was the 'office' of XJB 876, as driven to victory by the Morley twins in the French Alpine Rally of 1961. In those days, the long, direct-action, gearchange lever was still standard.

In 1961, most of the roads in the former Yugoslavia were as dusty and unwelcoming as this one. John Gott/ Bill Shepherd rush to keep up with an impossibly tight time schedule on the Liège-Sofia-Liège rally.

High speed, loose surfaces, searing temperatures – this can only be the Liège-Sofia-Liège marathon – 1961, with David Seigle-Morris on his way to sixth place.

Pat Moss/Ann Wisdom – both looking very tired – on the 1961 Liège-Sofia-Liège.

Peter Riley behind the wheel of his works 3000.

UJB 143 started life as a Warwick-built race car, then
became a works rally car – Pat Moss used it to win her
class in the 1961 Tour de Corse.

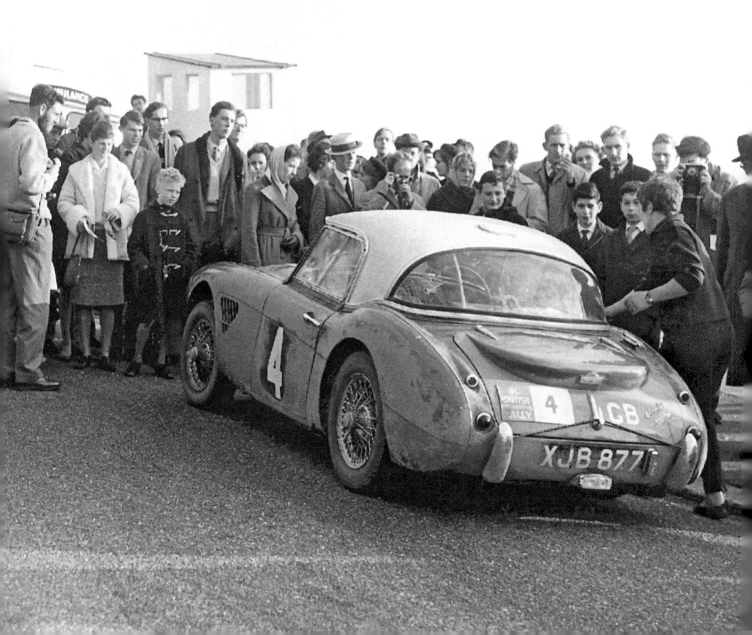

So near and yet ... Pat Moss finished second overall in the 1961 RAC Rally – beaten only by her husband-to-be (Erik Carlsson).

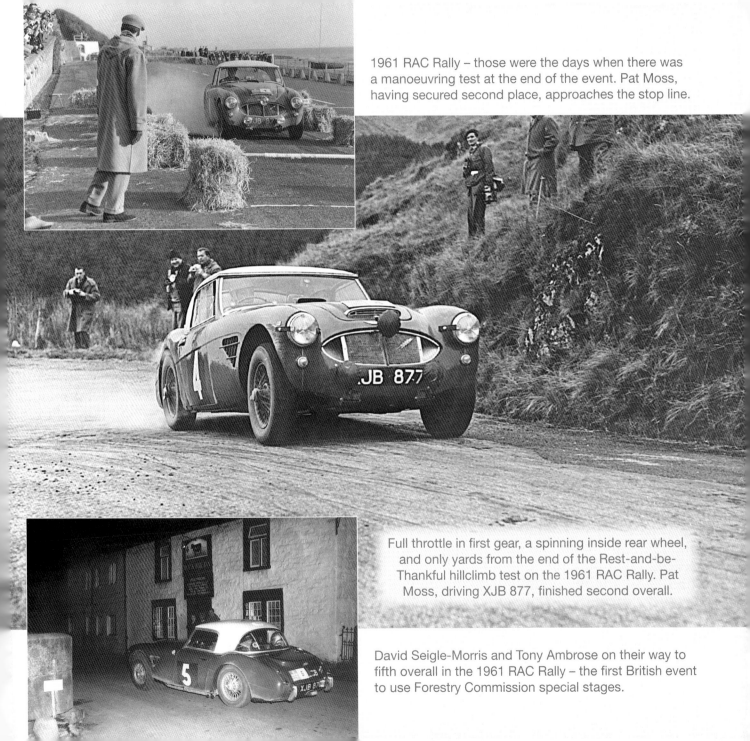

1961 RAC Rally – those were the days when there was a manoeuvring test at the end of the event. Pat Moss, having secured second place, approaches the stop line.

Full throttle in first gear, a spinning inside rear wheel, and only yards from the end of the Rest-and-be-Thankful hillclimb test on the 1961 RAC Rally. Pat Moss, driving XJB 877, finished second overall.

David Seigle-Morris and Tony Ambrose on their way to fifth overall in the 1961 RAC Rally – the first British event to use Forestry Commission special stages.

Snapshot of service, early 1960s style – with the Pat Moss/Ann Wisdom car receiving attention on the 1961 RAC.

than five near-identical works 3000s. It was an impressive effort, for all five of the 1961 cars – all the XJBs – took the start, the older cars having been used in advance for testing and for practice.

The line-up of works drivers had gradually been changing in the previous year, so on this occasion it was Pat Moss and the Morleys who were expected to set the pace, and for new-recruit David Seigle-Morris to provide the surprises.

As it happened, Lady Luck played against the team, though not entirely. Three of the five cars retired, all of

Pat Moss hurls XJB 877 into the final hairpin at the top of the Rest-and-be-Thankful speed hillclimb in the RAC Rally of 1961. She took second place.

Pat Moss, with her Healey 3000 in the 1961 RAC Rally.

them after accidents, that of Pat Moss ending up on its roof, with the hard-top well crushed. On the other hand, this was the first time that the redoubtable twins, Donald and Erle Morley, showed what was to become complete mastery of the high mountains of France and Italy. In a faultless performance, they kept their ex-Tulip Rally car (XJB 876) in one piece to win the event outright, while John Gott struggled on to take 15th overall in XJB 872.

The team's outing on the Liège-Sofia-Liège (this was the first time the event had struck deep into Bulgaria, by the way) was an almost complete disaster, when four of the ex-Alpine cars (only XJB 871 was not used again) took the start, but only one of them – that of David Seigle-Morris – made it to the finish.

There was no substitute for experience, it seemed. This was the first time the Liège's route returned from Bulgaria along the rocky, dusty, hot 'roads' (they were little better than tracks at times ...) of Jugoslavia's Adriatic coast. Two of the cars broke their rear suspension springs, another suffered a split sump, and in the end David Seigle-Morris (who had crashed his car at one point) was lucky to get his Healey to struggle back to Belgium.

At this point (and as already noted) there was a major change at Abingdon, where Marcus Chambers left the company, to be replaced by Stuart Turner. As far as the Healey programme was concerned, this would mean very little at first, though Turner soon made it clear that he wanted to hire new, younger and more (as he put it) 'beady-eyed' drivers for the future. Evolution of the Healey continued, and would not reach its peak until 1965.

At the end of the season, now under Turner's control,

BMC entered six cars in the RAC Rally, of which three were Healeys – XJB 870, XJB 876 and XJB 877. This was the first RAC to revolve around the use of high-speed special stages, most of them being run on Forestry Commission tracks. Although not as destructive as the Liège, this was an event where car/chassis strength was almost as significant as performance, and where traction was all important.

Although the Morleys' entry was out of luck – the car suffered from a broken rear hub bearing – the other two cars finished well-up. In the end, the only driver to beat Pat Moss was her husband-to-be, Erik Carlsson, in his front-wheel drive Saab 96. Pat's Healey set several fastest stage times, but the Carlsson/Saab combination was peerless where grip was lacking – and of course Erik was a phenomenally skilled driver on loose-surface events.

At the end of 1961, and soon after Stuart Turner had taken over from Marcus Chambers as BMC's competitions manager, a change in strategy at Abingdon was already seen to be on the way. Not only had there been a change at

Old Healeys rarely died – they were merely sold off, and sometimes re-registered. DG 95 was Don Grimshaw's car in 1962 – originally it had been SMO 745. This was Monte Carlo in 1962.

the top, but considerable changes in driver personnel soon followed, and as a result, team captain John Gott retired from rallying.

1962

Under Turner, sweeping changes to the team began in 1962. Paddy Hopkirk arrived in mid-season, and was shortly

David Seigle-Morris (left) and Tony Ambrose, with XJB 870, in which they won their class in the 1962 Monte Carlo Rally.

David Seigle-Morris joined the BMC team in 1960 from the Triumph team, and became a regular Big Healey driver for the next two seasons.

joined by Timo Makinen and Rauno Aaltonen. It was Timo and Rauno – the two original 'Flying Finns' – who were to have a pivotal effect on the fortunes of the Big Healey.

Paddy, incidentally, had been drawn to BMC from Rootes (it was his idea to move), specifically to get his hands on the 3000, but later he found the car much more difficult to drive than he had first thought. Paddy, like Pat Moss (another Superstar with no need to make excuses), also says that he was often frightened of the cars and their habits.

It's amazing how one could get the wrong idea from the sidelines. As a co-driver already in another works team at the time (Rootes), and about to run the re-born Triumph team, I recall most clearly that we assumed that the Mini Cooper was going to be BMC's future rally car, and that the Austin Healey 3000 had reached the limits of its development. How wrong we were!

For 1962, the works cars were back, faster, lighter and more effective than ever before. It wasn't just that the engineers at Abingdon had done more work, but that Stuart Turner, the new man at the top, had read the homologation regulations even more diligently than his predecessors had ever done. For the next few years, the performance of works

The works Competitions Department at Abingdon in 1962, with 47 ARX in the foreground, 67 ARX in the far corner, and another newly-prepared Healey 3000 being completed in the left foreground.

BMC competition cars owed as much to Stuart's reading of the rule book as it did to the designers themselves ...

The year started slowly, with David Seigle-Morris taking one of the 1961 models (XJB 870) on the Monte Carlo Rally, where the weather conditions were relatively mild, but where the organisers' complex handicapping system made it difficult for the big sports car to compete. David won his class, but could only finish 18th overall – and once again we wondered if this meant that the cars' competition life was coming to a close.

Then came the Tulip Rally, where most of the so-called 'secret' special stages were speed hillclimbs, which meant that sheer brute power was always going to be an advantage. Not only did BMC turn up for this event with two brand-new 3000s – 37 ARX and 47 ARX – but these had newly-developed engines, with light-alloy cylinder heads, and with three twin-choke Weber carburettors. The aluminium cylinder heads not only allowed higher compression ratios to be used, but they also reduced the cars' front end weight by 35lb, and even though this was nominally only a minor improvement, the drivers always insisted that it made the cars handle a little bit better than before. Maybe it did, and maybe it didn't – the weight reduction, after all, was not much more than one per cent overall, or perhaps two per cent over the front wheels – but if the drivers felt that way then it probably meant they drove a bit harder.

These days, of course, twin-choke Weber carburettors are old-hat to engine tuners, who are now deeply into the complexities of turbocharging and electronically controlled fuel injection systems, but at the beginning of the 1960s such instruments still looked fiendishly complex. They were still objects of mystery, held in awe by most engine builders outside Italy where they were produced. Weber, of course, was a long-established company, but the first sand-cast,

Two brand-new Healeys – 37 ARX (Morley twins, first in class) and 47 ARX (Peter Riley, second in class) – on their way to start a Tulip Rally special test in the 1962 Tulip Rally.

Peter Riley and Derek Astle took second in class in 47 ARX in the 1962 Tulip Rally – note that the access panel over the Weber carburettors has been removed.

The Morley twins, in 37 ARX, on the way to winning their capacity class in the 1962 Tulip – this car being the fastest machine on the rally, but hit hard by a handicapping system. Note that the access panel to the Weber carburettors has been removed.

Pace notes

By the time the 3000 became one of the world's best rally cars, 'pace notes' as prepared by crews in pre-event practice sessions, had become an integral part of a serious team's preparations. Notes of one form or another could give the conditions of the road or track ahead while not yet visible to the driver.

In spite of their fame, there is still much debate as to the origins of pace notes. Denis Jenkinson and John Fitch certainly used some notification in the 1954 Mille Miglia; Stirling Moss and Denis Jenkinson used a refined method when winning the 1955 Mille Miglia in a Mercedes-Benz 300SLR, and, by the end of the 1950s, some crude form of 'shouting up' existed between regular co-drivers and drivers.

BMC team manager Stuart Turner co-operated with John Sprinzel in preparing pace notes, for sale to Castrol runners, in events before he joined BMC – and by 1962 they had become part of the normal armoury of all serious competitors. Even so, until helmet-to-helmet intercoms were perfected in the late 1960s, a co-driver usually had to shout instructions across the car which, if the cabin was noisy, could be a very difficult operation.

side-draught, twin-choke Webers had not appeared until the early 1950s, when they were first used on Ferrari and Maserati single-seater racing cars.

Twin-choke Webers had first found use at BMC on a six-cylinder Austin Healey, a 1956 special car used for record breaking attempts in the USA, and were first homologated, then used, in Warwick-built racing cars in 1959, but had not hitherto been used on a works rally car. Nevertheless BMC's engineers, led by Abingdon's Doug Hamblin, took over an engine test bed at Abingdon, and rapidly established a new tune. Compared with the existing triple-2.0in. SU set-up. there was no torque advantage below 3000 rpm, but above this the initial runs showed progressive gains thereafter, and by the time the specification was settled the

Pat Moss and Pauline Mayman enjoying the Healey's performance in fine weather, on the way up the Mont Ventoux hillclimb in the 1962 French Alpine Rally, where they took third place.

team claimed 210bhp at 5750rpm. Naturally there were losses in the transmission and rear axle, so BMC's claim that there was 173bhp at 5600rpm at the rear wheels sounds very reasonable.

The engines and the details of the installation were still

One of the 1962 team cars – 67ARX – looking brand-new (or at least, extensively re-furbished) at Abingdon. This study shows the complex structural nature of the front end, and confirms that the front wings are bolt-on items.

Four works Healeys resting in the French sun, before tackling the Mont Ventoux speed hillclimb in the 1962 French Alpine Rally. The Morley twins won the event in 57 ARX, competition number 5 in this group.

Pat Moss and Pauline Mayman ready to start the French Alpine Rally of 1962, in 77 ARX, which was brand-new for this occasion.

47 ARX, one of the 1962-63 team cars, showing that there was a full-length undershield, and sturdy wire-mesh under the nose, to provide protection from the increasingly rough roads on the rallies of the early 1960s.

so new, that when Donald Morley and Peter Riley started the Tulip Rally, Doug Hamblin was still carrying pocketsful of carburettor jets with him, in case adjustments had to be made: indeed, some re-fettling of the carburettors took place during the event. But all the hard work (which included trips to Weber in Bologna, Italy along the way) was worth it in the end, and the Morleys set a stunning performance in the Tulip Rally, quite fast enough to have won the event outright if the rally had been run on 'real time'. As it was, the

Halfway up a speed hillclimb in the mountains, this is Pat Moss on her way to third place in the 1962 French Alpine Rally.

Logan Morrison's Healey lined up in Liège, ready to start the Liège-Sofia-Liège four-day marathon to and from the Bulgarian capital.

complicated class-improvement handicap system was still in place, which meant that the Morleys had to be content with a class victory, while Pat Moss used a much slower 997cc Mini Cooper to claim outright victory.

Later in the season, Abingdon completed the new set of five 'ARX' cars, which went on to lead an eventful life for the next two seasons before they were gradually supplanted by BJ8 MkIII types. These days, cars that survive are now cosseted, and look magnificent, but, at the time, every works

Big Healey tended to have a hard working life, either as a rally car, or as a practice machine (and those were the days when practice meant just that – with the cars being driven hard and fast, for days on end).

Because international rallies were getting rougher and more demanding all the time – of the major events which the Healeys tackled, only the Tulip and the Alpine were run entirely on tarmac surfaces – this meant that the rugged chassis/inner structure tended to have a very hard time, and

Spa-Sofia-Liège

Without detailing the route of one of the final events in this amazing marathon rally, it is difficult to convey just how difficult and gruelling such races could be.

Although the event was organised by the Royal Motor Union, of Liège, Belgium, in the last two years of its open-road existence (1963 and 1964), the actual route started from Spa, a town some miles away; the same Spa which gives its name to famous F1 race circuit. In 1964 the route totalled no less than 3100 miles, and covered four days and nights, with no overnight rest halt.

The event started from Spa on Tuesday evening, 25 August, running through West Germany and the Italian Dolomites, before entering what was still Yugoslavia from Tarvisio on the Wednesday evening. The hard work, rough roads and high average speeds then began, the route passing through what is now Croatia, Bosnia, and Serbia before reaching Sofia, the capital of Bulgaria.

After two difficult days and nights, the crews were allowed just one hour in Sofia for a meal and maybe a shower, before setting off back for the even more gruelling run around the northern borders of Albania to Titograd, then up the awful tracks in the mountains behind the Adriatic coast, before finally re-entering Italy at Gorizia, late on the third afternoon. Then, the highest passes of the Italian Dolomites (including the horrid passes of the Gavia, Vivione and Stelvio) had to be tackled during the night, before the last, tedious fourth day's run involved a long trek back up the Austrian and German autobahns, to arrive in Liège on the Saturday evening.

Anyone insisting that they had not needed wakey-wakey pills, or were not exhausted, was lying, for cars and crews were totally worn out afterwards. In 1964, the winning Healey lost just 57 minutes on an impossible time schedule, beating Carlsson's remarkable Saab by 28 minutes, and the redoubtable Eugen Bohringer's Mercedes-Benz 230SL by 30 minutes.

sometimes suffered a lot. It was normal for one of these cars to tackle no more than two or, at the most, three events before its chassis/inner structure had to be discarded, after which the 'old' car, carrying an existing identity, was reborn around a new structure with many new items of running gear, too.

This was the period, however, in which these cars genuinely took on the

Logan Morrison and the Rev Rupert Jones, assaulting the Moistrocca pass, close to the Italian-Yugoslavian (Slovenian) border in the 1962 Liège-Sofia-Liège rally – they took fifth overall.

Paddy Hopkirk enjoying a power slide at Oulton Park during the 1962 RAC Rally – he finished second to Erik Carlsson's phenomenal Saab.

aura of rallying supercars. With their red paintwork, always allied to white hard-tops, they always looked magnificent, and enthusiasts used to salivate over the details of their preparation – the humped boot lid to allow two spare wheels to be fitted, the side exhaust outlets to optimise the ground clearance, and the detachable panel in the bonnet surround which gave access to the twin-choke Weber carburettors.

More importantly, there was the glamour which developed around the cars' extrovert character. Peter Riley, at the time one of the team's drivers, always said that, even in later years, when the engine of a works 3000 was fired up in the workshops at Abingdon, most people would stop work, suspend their own private conversations, turn towards the noise, and beam fondly. When it was sitting on the start line, ready to start a special stage, a Big Healey would be burbling away to itself, with that unmistakeable and uneven exhaust note which someone once likened to the emptying of an old-style bath tub. Out on the stages themselves, there was never any doubt that a 3000 was approaching, for the combination of exhaust noise, Weber carburettor gobble, and the crashing and banging underneath as the skid shields contacted the unmade surfaces, was always recognisable.

The romance, in fact, was mainly

Pat Moss and Paul Mayman at the start of the 1962 RAC Rally – this being the first occasion on which works Healeys used auxiliary headlamps mounted inboard of the standard items.

Pat Moss' very last drive for BMC came in 77 ARX, in the 1962 RAC Rally, where she took third overall.

on the outside, for there is no doubt that the cars were hard work to drive fast, very noisy in the cabin, and they got very hot indeed in the cockpit, too. In 1962, remember, pace notes might have been present, but driver-to-co-driver intercoms were still not in general use (Paul Easter remembers that he could have used one of these, with Timo Makinen, by 1965, but that Timo refused to listen).

This meant that co-drivers like Erle Morley and Ann

XXXII° Rallye de Monte Carlo 1963

In January 1963, BMC paired Timo Makinen and Christabel Carlisle to drive this works Healey 3000 in the Monte Carlo Rally. Amazingly, Timo kept it on the road to win his capacity class.

Even with studded Dunlop tyres, Healeys understeered violently on ice and snow! Timo Makinen/Christabel Carlisle won their class in 77 ARX In the '63 Monte Carlo Rally.

Wisdom had to shout themselves hoarse to be understood, and sometimes detailed instructions were abandoned. Erle once showed me his notes for an ultra-fast hillclimb in the French Alps which details a tight bend, followed by a hairpin, followed by the memorable phrase "now fast for the next three miles."

There was really no solution to the hot cockpit problem, for the cars always ran with hard-tops and sidescreens in place. The small roof vent (ex-Austin van, apparently) was more of a recognition of the problem, rather than an effective addition. Heat transfer through the passenger bulkhead, from the engine bay, was immense, and for the co-driver, who had to sit on top of the side-mounted exhaust silencer, the Big Healey provided a real sauna treatment. On a car which had been in the wars a little, and which leaked cold air around the door seals, this was not an ideal environment. Did you ever see an overweight Austin Healey co-driver? Of course not!

After winning the Tulip in a Mini Cooper, Pat Moss went off on the Greek Acropolis Rally, where she finished eighth and won her capacity class, in XJB 877, but the highlight of the season was what followed on the French Alpine.

For this summer mountain pass-storming classic, where cars had to battle not only with high-altitude passes and demanding schedules, but with normal traffic too, not only did Turner enter four Healeys – 47 ARX, 57 ARX, 67 ARX and 77 ARX – but it proved to be another win for the Morley twins (in 57 ARX), with Pat Moss taking third place, and David Seigle-Morris eighth. Only Peter Riley, who went off

the road on the high-speed trial at the Italian Monza test, failed to finish, which was certainly not the car's fault.

Pat Moss gained second place on the Polish (in 77 ARX, her ex-Alpine car), but the team's showing in the Liège-Sofia-Liège Marathon which followed in September was only a partial success. Two of the four Healeys retired – one of them (Paddy Hopkirk's car) with a broken rear spring, which was something of an habitual failing on Healeys when the going was rough, another (Rauno Aaltonen's entry) when the crew lost their rally roadbook (this, it seems, being stolen by a souvenir hunter at a time control). On the other hand, Logan Morrison finished fifth, and David Seigle-Morris eighth on an event which proved to be ferociously rough, fast, and car-breaking: even for the Healey, it seemed, there were limits to its pace and endurance on bad roads, and the cars which finished ahead of it were all saloons with higher ground clearance, if not more performance.

Traditionally, as ever, the season ended with a four-Healey entry in the RAC Rally, where none of the Healeys could quite keep up with the flying Erik Carlsson in his front-wheel drive Saab 96: although Erik had recently married Pat Moss, he was not about to give way to her or to any of her team mates in a major rally. The result was that the Healeys finished second (Paddy Hopkirk, in 67 ARX) and third (Pat Moss, 77 ARX).

1963

In 1963 the Mini Cooper S came on to the rally scene at Abingdon; this was

Looking more familiar, and more relaxed, on asphalt, this was Timo Makinen's works Healey on the Monaco GP circuit at the close of the 1963 Monte Carlo Rally, where he won his class.

By the time that 77 ARX reached Monte Carlo at the end of the 1963 rally, it had already completed four major international rallies.

such an outstanding little rally car that, in publicity terms, the works 3000s were rather pushed out of the limelight. It was a season when they did not record a single outright victory, even though they were undoubtedly capable of that. In fairness, after the Weber-carburetted specification had settled down – which it did, during 1963 – the works Healeys never got any quicker in straight-line performance, they merely seemed to become more reliable, and even more likely to finish any rally unless pushed beyond all reasonable endurance.

Amazingly, BMC made a Healey entry in the Monte Carlo Rally, for Timo Makinen and Christabel Carlisle to drive (this winter classic was hardly the most suitable for a 200bhp-plus sports car to tackle), and even more amazingly,

Timo wrestled the car through blizzard-like conditions – it really was one of the bleakest Montes of all time – to finish thirteenth overall, and win his capacity class. (According to BMC legend, this event goes down on record, they say, as being the only occasion on which any of Timo's co-drivers – Christabel in this case – ever urged the brave and tempestuous Finnish driver to go faster! Maybe I should not write 'legend', for Christabel has told me, more than once, that she really was naïve enough to make that suggestion.)

By this time, BMC was so depressed by the attitude of the Tulip Rally organisers to high performance cars, that it only sent two Healeys to tackle the 1963 event. As usual, need I say, the Morley twins/Healey/37ARX combination

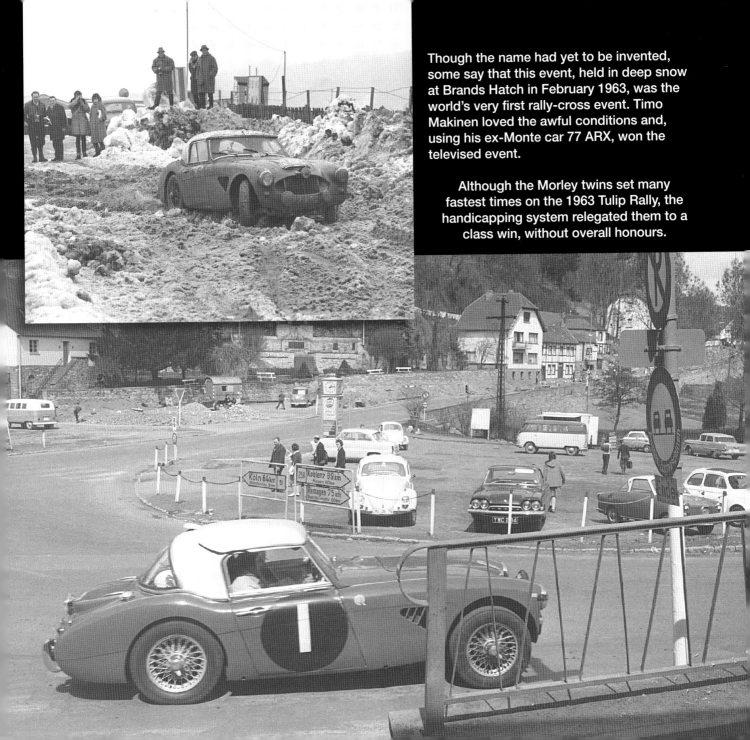

Though the name had yet to be invented, some say that this event, held in deep snow at Brands Hatch in February 1963, was the world's very first rally-cross event. Timo Makinen loved the awful conditions and, using his ex-Monte car 77 ARX, won the televised event.

Although the Morley twins set many fastest times on the 1963 Tulip Rally, the handicapping system relegated them to a class win, without overall honours.

This service halt on the 1963 French Alpine Rally sees Timo Makinen's car (57 ARX) with Stuart Turner (in specs) talking to the Morley twins and Logan Morrison (red shirt).

Story without words! Timo Makinen's car (competition number 2, 57 ARX) has crashed into a large logging truck on the Spa-Sofia-Liège rally, and now everyone is wondering how to retrieve the stricken machine.

Radiator stoved in, front suspension wrecked, chassis bent, and engine out of commission – no wonder Timo Makinen's car had to retire after this 1963 Spa-Sofia-Liège crash, head-on, into a truck. The car had to be written off when it eventually returned to the UK.

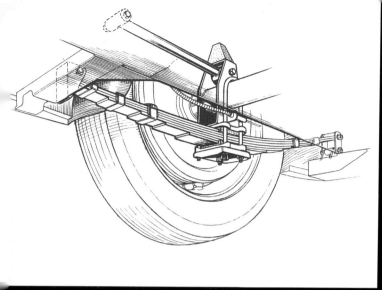

Tried out by the works team in the 1963 Spa-Sofia-Liège, and fitted to all BJ8s from the spring of 1964, the 3000's rear suspension featured twin trailing arms instead of a Panhard rod location.

Rauno Aaltonen and Tony Ambrose were well on course to win the Spa-Sofia-Liège marathon of 1963, driving 77 ARX, before they crashed on the Passo di Gavia.

On the 1963 RAC Rally, the Morley twins put in another steady performance, finishing 9th in 67 ARX.

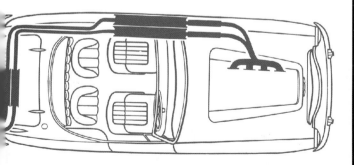

From 1964, all BJ8 road cars had twin 2.0in SU carburettors, and the final sturdy type of gearchange. In that form, they produced 148bhp, whereas a specially-prepared works rally engine would have at least 210bhp.

This drawing shows the sinuous routing of BJ8 exhaust systems, and why the works cars tended to have pipes cut off immediately behind the main silencers; this reduced weight, and made the pipes less vulnerable to underbody damage.

ARX 91B was the very first works BJ8 (the wind-up window variety of 3000), and Paddy Hopkirk used it to win the 1964 Austrian Alpine Rally. All of the BJ8 works cars had extra headlamps mounted in nacelles.

were the fastest overall, but they were awarded with only a class win for their efforts.

Unhappily, all four cars retired from the French Alpine Rally (which was a real downer, following two previous outright wins in that event). The time schedule was more demanding than ever, two cars were eliminated in accidents, one (Timo's) broke a front stub axle, while the Morleys suffered a truly cruel blow ...

Looking to be un-penalised for the third successive year on road sections (which would have resulted in them winning a Coupe d'Or), they were thwarted by the failure of the limited slip differential (this was the first time such a fitting had been used), which suffered a breakage at the start of the Col d'Allos speed hillclimb.

Of the four cars that started Spa-Sofia-Liège (this was the usual Marathon, slightly re-titled), only Paddy Hopkirk finished the event, in sixth place, after two others crashed in Yugoslavia, and after Rauno Aaltonen crashed his car on the Col du Vivione, in northern Italy, on the final night, while leading the event. Rauno and co-driver Tony Ambrose, it seems, were lucky to escape with their lives, for the car wedged itself over the edge of a sheer drop!

There wasn't even the consolation of a good result in the end-of-season RAC Rally, where three Healeys started, two finished, and Timo Makinen could finish no higher than fifth (and win his class) in a car which had split its gearbox casing, and was only just able to reach the finish line while consuming gallons of transmission oil.

1964

In 1964 the Mini Cooper S took even more attention from

Tony Ambrose was Rauno Aaltonen's co-driver on many rallies, including the famous occasion when they won the Spa-Sofia-Liège rally in 1964.

Paddy Hopkirk/Henry Liddon on their way to winning the 1964 Austrian Alpine Rally in ARX 91B.

By 1964, BMC was using an extra fuel bowser, towed behind one of its Austin A99 service barges, to use in the depths of the Balkans in the Spa-Sofia-Liège rally.

Was this the Big Healey's best victory? Certainly Rauno Aaltonen and Tony Ambrose pulverised all the opposition in the 1964 Spa-Sofia-Liège rallies, using this brand-new BJ8-based 3000.

Not all works-supported Healeys were rally cars. 57 FAC was one of several prepared for racing in North America, by Healey itself, at its workshops in Warwick.

This magnificent shot shows Rauno Aaltonen's Healey in full flight, on a loose-surfaced track, on its way to winning the Spa-Sofia-Liège Rally of 1964. If only we had a soundtrack, too ...

the team (especially after Paddy Hopkirk won the Monte Carlo Rally, a feat which resulted in his car being flown home to appear on a prime-time Sunday evening TV show). Even so, this was also the year in which new wind-up window BJ8-style works Healeys were commissioned, and when the Healey notched up two outright victories – one for Paddy Hopkirk in the Austrian Alpine, the other in altogether more dramatic circumstances in the last Spa-Sofia-Liège of all.

In May the Morleys set their habitual fastest scratch performance in the Tulip (using ARX 92B, a new BJ8), and as usual they were cheated from outright victory by that event's handicap marking system. Only weeks later they took the same car out on the French Alpine Rally, where they had better luck than in 1963, finishing with a fine class win.

Even so, it was in the Spa-Sofia-Liège event of 1964 that the 3000's reputation as the outstanding rally car of its generation was confirmed for all

Close to the end of the gruelling RAC Rally of 1964, the Morley twins' BJ8-based works 3000, BMO 93B (the same car had won the Spa-Sofia-Liège) shows that it had been off road for a long time on one special stage.

The Morleys in their works 3000 hustling downhill on the Porlock special stage in the 1964 RAC Rally.

time. Using a brand-new BJ8 model (registered BMO 93B), Rauno Aaltonen and Tony Ambrose won the last, the fastest and the toughest edition of this justly famous Belgian-organised event. Although they completely dominated the event, eventually winning by 30 minutes, they had to drive to the very limits of their own, and the car's endurance, to achieve this.

Co-driver Tony Ambrose later recalled that he had driven almost half the mileage (including some of the tough sections, for Rauno Aaltonen became exhausted close to the end) but that, naturally, Rauno had driven almost all the impossible sections. The car, need one say, behaved beautifully, even though both crew members had high-speed incidents in it. The two other team cars both retired, and only 21 of the original 98 starters made it back to the finish in Belgium.

After BMO 93B had won Spa-Sofia-Liège in 1964, BMC re-prepared it for the Morleys to drive in the RAC Rally, where it finished twenty-first.

Although Rauno Aaltonen and Tony Ambrose won the 1964 Spa-Sofia-Liège in BMO 93B, the car looks so immaculate here that the picture must have been taken at a very early stage of the event.

Using this brand-new 3000, the Morley twins set the fastest possible times on the 1965 Tulip Rally through, as usual, a handicapping system demoted them to eighth overall.

Service on the Tulip Rally of 1965 for the Morley twins. Peter Browning, who would become competitions manager in 1967, is talking to Erle Morley on the left of the car. The author (in spectacles) is leaning into the car, talking to driver Donald Morley.

This 1964-built 3000, originally a rally car, was re-prepared at Abingdon to go racing in 1965 – in the Targa Florio (where it finished 20th), and in the Guards 1000 race at Brands Hatch , where Paddy Hopkirk and Roger Mac finished fourth overall.

Only Timo Makinen would get a Healey as sideways as this – Scottish Rally 1965 when he was leading – but the car eventually broke under the strain.

After this, another fine performance by Timo Makinen in the RAC Rally – where he took second place in BRX 852B, to a superbly driven Volvo piloted by Tom Trana – went almost unnoticed.

1965

By 1965 the 3000s were close to their peak, but were rapidly coming to the end of their front-line careers. Even if rallying's Appendix J regulations (which governed homologation) had not been due for revision, the Healeys were already being outpaced on several types of event by the incredible performance of the works Mini Cooper S saloons. It wasn't just that the Minis were equally as fast on loose surfaces, or on ice and snow, but that they were so much easier to drive fast, so much quicker and cheaper to repair (and to rebuild after a shunt!). All of this meant that more entries, with a greater chance of victory, could be placed in a given year. Team manager Stuart Turner was, above all, a financial realist, knew that his BMC marketing bosses were anxious to keep the Mini in the headlines, and gradually allowed the 3000s to fade into the background.

The proposed changes in Appendix J regulations had serious implications for the Big Healey. In an attempt to reduce the cost of motorsport and to make it easier for private owners to

The Big Healey on its last-ever French Alpine Rally, where the Morleys took DRX 258C to a fine class win.

The Morley twins – Donald driving, Erle the co-driver – in the French Alpine of 1965 in this brand-new 3000. The result was a class win.

compete against factory cars (how many times have we heard those fine words, before and since?) the sport's governing body decided to cut down on authorised options and allowances – and, in particular, to ban the use of alternative cylinder heads, the use of non-homologated carburation, the use of alternative body panel materials, and to insist that items like bumpers should always be fitted to cars. All these changes would take effect on 1 January 1966.

Such rules might have been written specifically to outlaw the famous works Austin Healeys, though in fairness they also pulled the teeth of cars like the exotically-specified works Triumph Spitfires, the MG Midgets, some of the Porsches, and did nothing for the competitiveness of the MGBs. At a stroke this meant that further development work on the 3000s had to be stopped – works cars would only appear on six events in 1965 (and even then, with the single exception of the RAC Rally, these were only singleton entries) – and the fleet was rapidly run down.

A week after it had won its class in the 1965 French Alpine, DRX 258C found itself used as an ordinary road car by *Autocar* magazine. The writer actually used if for commuting for several days!

Preparation work at Abingdon before the Big Healey's last-ever works appearance in November 1965 on the RAC Rally. Centre left is EJB 806C, new for Timo Makinen to drive in the RAC Rally, and in the far distance is DRX258C, which the Morleys would drive.

As was traditional, the Morley twins drove one of the cars in the Tulip Rally, and, as was equally traditional, they set a series of fastest stage and hillclimb times, though yet again, an unfavourable handicap marking system reduced them to eighth overall in the standings. Abingdon then entered ARX 91B in the Targa Florio race in Sicily, for Timo Makinen

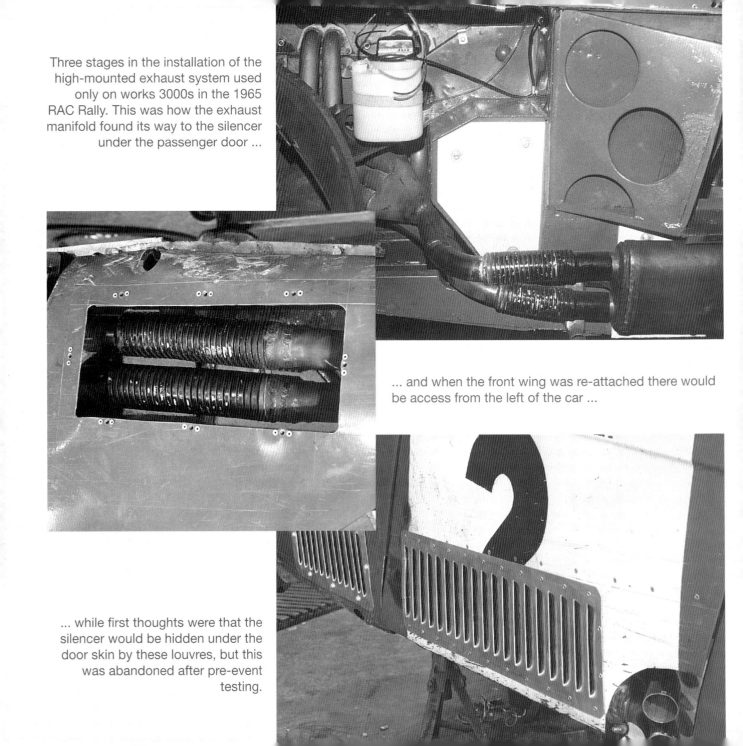

Three stages in the installation of the high-mounted exhaust system used only on works 3000s in the 1965 RAC Rally. This was how the exhaust manifold found its way to the silencer under the passenger door ...

... and when the front wing was re-attached there would be access from the left of the car ...

... while first thoughts were that the silencer would be hidden under the door skin by these louvres, but this was abandoned after pre-event testing.

The Morleys' Healey at the Oulton Park special stage in the 1965 RAC Rally.

and Paul Hawkins to drive. This might have made marketing and publicity sense, but little else; the gallant old recce car led its class for three long laps, lost half an hour when a distributor component came loose, and finished 20th.

A few weeks later, Timo and Paul Easter entered the Scottish Rally, which featured hot weather and lots of rough special stages. Timo drove in his usual ultra-rapid and extrovert style (the published photographs prove just how

Ice and hard-packed snow were not ideal conditions for a Healey, even though Finnish hero Timo Makinen was driving the car. This was the RAC Rally of 1965.

On Timo Makinen's last outing in a Healey, he drove his car up to, and beyond, the limit on several occasions. Here is a sneak picture to prove the point.

hard he was driving), but along the way the car damaged its sump guard, broke its distributor (again!), and finally broke its rear axle final drive before having to retire.

The Morleys were more fortunate on the Geneva Rally, finishing seventh overall in spite of fighting yet another unfavourable handicap, while on the Alpine Rally they used the same car to finish second in the entire GT category, one minute behind Bernard Consten's Alfa Romeo Giulia GTZ, which was really a racing sports car. One way or another, the Big Healey was being squeezed out of contention – either by modern rallying trends, or by very specialised new models.

The last event tackled in 1965 (and due to the imminent application of new regulations for 1966, the last for which the Healey could be competitive) was Britain's RAC Rally, an event which the Austin Healey had never won in all those years of trying. With Timo Makinen and Donald Morley both anxious to end the car's career with a flourish, Abingdon made a real effort to tailor the cars to the conditions; while nothing more could be done to make the cars faster, to give them more traction, or to make them handle better on this event, perhaps there was still one way to make them less vulnerable to under-car damage of the exhaust system ...

Surprisingly enough, in his seminal book on BMC's Competitions Department, Bill Price makes little of the work which went into providing a new, high, exhaust system, for which mechanic Nobby Hall takes most of the credit, yet it involved major structural change. The theory, clearly, was that if the chassis/body unit itself could not be lifted higher off the ground, then ways had to be found to lift the vulnerable silencer further. After a great deal of deliberation, it was decided to raise the silencer by several inches, positioning this up the side of the bodywork, underneath a passenger's door which had been made more shallow, while doing as much as possible to get the heat away from the cabin. At the same time, the sump guards were actually welded, not bolted into position.

Looking back, with an independent eye (though, I admit, I was running a rival team in this period, and paying just as close attention to Appendix J regulations!), I am by no means certain that the major structural changes quite complied with Appendix J regulations. To accommodate the raised system and the raised silencer, major surgery was needed on the front inner and outer wings, the bulkhead, the floor and the passenger door itself – but the RAC's scrutineers did not reject the layout. The first version, first tried out in private testing on Timo Makinen's ex-Scottish

Opposite. At one point in Timo Makinen's meteoric drive to finish second in the
1965 RAC Rally, his starter motor failed. Much pushing, therefore, was needed to
get him going again after a halt for repairs in the depths of Yorkshire. The writer (in
spectacles and a duffle coat) is pushing from the back of the car.

Several small accidents later (look at the profile of the front wing, and the driver's door!) the Makinen/Healey 3000
is still on its way to second place in the 1965 RAC Rally.

Rally machine (DRX 257C) had its silencer behind louvres in the door panel, while the definitive system (with an exposed silencer), was used on the RAC cars themselves (DRX 258C, Donald Morley's ex-Alpine Rally car, and a brand new machine, EJB 806C), where the silencer was positioned out in the open to maximise the cooling effect.

There were two exhaust outlet pipes which pumped out hot gases at wheel hub height – which was also almost exactly the right height to embarrass the marshals who were issuing or collecting time cards on the left side of the cars at rally controls!

The looks, and the noise, of the special machines were exciting enough, but once the event got under way it was Makinen's driving which caught the media's attention. While the Morleys lost 30 minutes after their rear axle failed, Timo overcame awfully slippery conditions, occasional off-road excursions, a flat battery, and a full-blooded blizzard in the Yorkshire stages, to lead the event until the closing hours. At one point, team manager Stuart Turner had mechanics scouring pet shops in Yorkshire towns, buying up dog leads to turn into impromptu tyre chains!

The Morleys retired when they crashed in Loch Achray forest, while Timo thundered on, despite getting stuck in the snow on more than one occasion. By the end of the event neither of the car's doors fitted properly any more, almost every panel had been creased against snow banks, trees – or even other competitors – and it was on a slippery stage in Wales that his car ground to a halt, to be passed (on the road, and in penalties) by his team-mate and rival Rauno Aaltonen (Mini Cooper 1275S).

Although Rauno finally beat Timo by 3min 8sec, it tells us everything about Timo's (and the Healey's) performance, that he set 28 fastest stage times, 11 second fastests and three third fastests – but that he also suffered from two maximum penalties. Rally winner Aaltonen, in a Mini Cooper 1275S, was only fastest on 10 occasions – but had no maximum penalties.

1967

That should have been the last we ever saw of a works

Big Healey, for at the end of the 1965 season all seven of the MkIIIs were either sold off, or in the case of DRX 257C, the ex-Scottish/ex-high-exhaust test car, scrapped.

But that wasn't quite the end. Two years after these cars had last tackled an international rally, one final attempt was proposed to win the RAC Rally, for the 1964 and 1965 failures still rankled with the works team. In 1967, for the first time, the organisers of the event decided to include a category for non-homologated prototypes – FIA Group 6 machines, which meant that a Big Healey (which was then very close to the end of its life as a production car – that date was only weeks away) might once again be made competitive.

Any number of such special cars were entered by various manufacturers, but the most exciting of all was undoubtedly a single works Austin Healey 3000, for Rauno Aaltonen and Henry Liddon to drive.

This was to be no run-of-the-mill rally car, for Abingdon was determined to pour in all the expertise that it could re-create from the past – and some which had never before been applied to a 3000.

In mid-1967, though, there was a problem in that Abingdon no longer held any 3000s on its fleet. Accordingly, it was an ageing 1964 MkIII team car (ARX 92B), which had been sold off at the end of 1965 to Peter Browning, which was made available. Peter, who had succeeded Stuart Turner as BMC's competitions manager early in 1967, had re-registered it PWB 57 for his own road car use, and was 'persuaded' (his description) to loan it back to the company for this event.

As Peter later wrote: "The car was probably the most powerful road-going 3000 ever built. An all-aluminium engine [this was basically the same as planned for use in the MG MGC GTS race cars] was fitted, bored out to 2968cc,

Opposite: The fastest and best works Healey of all never started a rally! This was the car, originally registered as ARX 92B, but later carrying Peter Browning's personal plate, which was prepared for the 1967 RAC Rally, an event that was cancelled the day before the start.

Big Healeys never die! Even as late as 1991, Stirling Moss and Zoe Heritage used this car to compete in the Pirelli Classic Marathon. Roger Clark, who was to drive a Ford, wished he could get behind the wheel of the Healey, too.

with three 45 DCOE Weber carburettors, giving a power output of nearly 200bhp at the wheels! Despite extensive lightening, the additional load of rally gear, sump and underside guards, etc, brought the weight up to just 24cwt [2688lb/1219kg], which was carried on four sturdy Minilite magnesium alloy wheels shod with Dunlop 185-15 SP44 radial Weathermaster tyres."

Naturally it was given a developed version of the high-side-exhaust system, this time with the silencer hidden behind louvres in the full-length outer door skin

When the RAC ran the Golden 50 Rally in 1982, Philip Young entered this re-registered ex-works Healey (it used to be SJB 471), with Jack Sears driving the car on the race circuits. Doors that opened involuntarily were always a hazard with tired old Healeys!

panel. This was also the first, and only, works Healey rally car to be equipped with dual circuit brakes and twin vacuum servo units, and because the engine was much lighter than the standard unit (about 100lb/45kg some say), this car was found to handle much better than any of its predecessors.

Incidentally, because the registration number of this particular car was over three years old when it was finally ready to tackle the rally, it had to be driven down to the local testing station to pass a mandatory MoT test! During the 1970s, that also happened to so-called three-year-old works Escorts on occasion.

The result was magnificent and, according to the form book, it should have been a winning car, but on the evening before the start of the event, when the car had already gone through pre-event scrutineering, the rally was cancelled. A very serious outbreak of foot-and-mouth disease (which affects animals with cloven hoofs) was sweeping through the British countryside, and since this disease was easily transmitted by the tyres and undersides of cars, there was no way that the event could be allowed to go ahead.

The world's finest Austin Healey 3000 rally car, therefore, never even started an event, was returned to Peter Browning in 'as-prepared' condition (naturally he was delighted to receive it in such a fresh state!), and was eventually sold off to Arthur Carter, a secretive collector in East Anglia. Perhaps it was fitting that production of Austin Healey 3000s came to an end just weeks after the RAC Rally of 1967 was cancelled.

After that, BMC's rally efforts seemed to crumble, for following the foundation of British Leyland, the company's motorsport policy changed completely. There was no obvious successor to the 3000, and the next ultra-fast sports car to go rallying was the Triumph TR7 V8, of 1978-1980.

1965: was the Big Healey at its limit?

Although the impending change in Appendix J Homologation rules meant that the Healey, in its ultimate works rally form – light-alloy body, aluminium cylinder head, high-mounted exhaust system and all – was due to

be banned at the end of 1965, this came at a time when the car had really reached its development limits, though the road car would stay in production for two more seasons.

Looking back, even without the homologation changes, it is difficult to see how many more mechanical improvements could have been made to the existing rally car – changes, that is, which would all have to be homologated. Engine power, in fact, had stalled at about 210bhp since 1962/63, the gearbox specification had settled down, and the limited-slip differential had finally been made reliable.

There could be no further changes to improve the chassis' performance on unmade roads – especially to provide increased rear axle movement and better traction – for the BJ8 road car already incorporated the re-profiled side members and an increase in ground clearance. Further, the exhaust system had already been placed in its optimum (raised) position, and no further improvements could be expected in that area.

To improve the handling, wider wheels and tyres would have helped a little, but flared wheelarches to suit were not authorised by the regulations – they could only have been added if every road car was built in the same way.

The definitive BJ8 of 1965, accordingly, was as good a rally car as it could possibly be. The prototype conversion job made for the cancelled RAC Rally of 1967 proved this point, for every change was made outside the rules governing the homologation of the machine.

Mission impossible? A successor to the Big Healey?

If BMC had not become British Leyland in 1968, and if the new bosses at British Leyland had even seemed to understand what motorsport (rallying in particular) was all about, the works team at Abingdon might have been able to develop a worthy successor to the Healey.

Potentially, there was such a car – the much-discussed lightweight MGC GTS – which showed promise, but which was never backed with any conviction by top management. First under Stuart Turner, then under Peter Browning, plans were laid to make the 6-cylinder MGC GT into a lightweight,

Afterlife! Historic rally enthusiast Philip Young hurls his ex-works 3000 up a hill in India in a Himalayas Rally of the 1980s.

In 1989 racing legend Stirling Moss drove this Austin Healey 3000 in the Pirelli Classic Marathon – and enjoyed the event, in spite of nibbling the front offside wing at one point!

ultra-powerful, ultra-specialised race car, but in the end just two non-homologated prototype machines were built in 1968 and 1969.

On Peter Browning's wish-list, a lightweight car – tentatively titled MGC GTS – would have been put into minimum production (Pressed Steel Fisher was already producing the basic steel shells at Swindon, just a few miles down the road from Abingdon), as would an aluminium-blocked version of the 2.9-litre 6-cylinder engine from that car. The handling was not good at first, but remedies were being developed, and there seemed to be little doubt that the definitive MGC GTS could have been a better car that the Healey 3000 had ever been. Even so, it might have been

an uphill struggle, for by 1969 Porsche's rear-engined 911S had already become a formidable machine, while the tiny, fragile, but increasingly reliable Alpine-Renault was proving to be astonishing fast on most surfaces.

Unhappily, this project was fated not to come to fruition, so after the Sebring 12-hour race of March 1969 (where both MGC GTS cars competed), that programme was wound down. It would not be until 1978 that Abingdon once again ran a competitive two-seater rally car – the TR7 V8 – and that never reached the heights of its illustrious ancestor.

Major European rally successes

Event	Position	Car	Drivers
1958			
Liège-Rome-Liège	4th	PMO 201 (100-Six)	Ms P Moss/Ms A Wisdom
– all subsequent success was in 3000 models.			
1959			
Liège-Rome-Liège	3rd	SMO 744	P Riley/R Jones
Germany	2nd	SMO 746	Ms P Moss/Ms A Wisdom
RAC	4th	SMO 745	D Morley/E Morley
1960			
French Alpine	2nd	URX 727	Ms P Moss/Ms A Wisdom
Liège-Rome-Liège	1st	URX 727	Ms P Moss/Ms A Wisdom
RAC	3rd	SJB 471	D Morley/E Morley
1961			
Acropolis	3rd	XJB 871	P Riley/A Ambrose
French Alpine	1st	XJB 876	D Morley/E Morley
RAC	2nd	XJB 877	Ms P Moss/Ms A Wisdom
1962			
French Alpine	1st	57 ARX	D.Morley/E.Morley
	3rd	77 ARX	Ms P Moss/Ms P Mayman
Polish	2nd	77 ARX	Ms P Moss/Ms P Mayman
RAC	2nd	67 ARX	P Hopkirk/J Scott
	3rd	77 ARX	Ms P Moss/Ms P Mayman
1963			
Tulip	2nd Cat.	37 ARX	D Morley/E Morley

Event	Position	Car	Drivers
1964			
Tulip	1st Cat.	ARX 92B	D Morley/E Morley
Austrian Alpine	1st	ARX 91B	P Hopkirk/H Liddon
French Alpine	2nd Cat.	ARX 92B	D Morley/E Morley
Spa-Sofia-Liège	1st	BMO 93B	R Aaltonen/A Ambrose
RAC	2nd	BRX 852B	T Makinen/D Barrow
1965			
French Alpine	2nd Cat.	DRX 258C	D Morley/E Morley
RAC	2nd	EJB 806C	T Makinen/P Easter

Works rally cars (and when first used)

These are the identities of the factory-prepared six-cylinder Austin Healey rally cars built and registered by BMC (British Motor Corporation) between 1957 and 1967, for use in major European events. In each case I have listed the first year in which they appeared. Note that as structures wore out, or were crashed, some of these identities were 'cloned', and re-appeared on newly-built cars.

Where applicable, I have added important successes.

1957
Austin Healey 100-Six
UOC 741

1958
PMO 201 (4th, 1958 Liège-Rome-Liège)
PMO 202
PMO 203 (converted to 3000 spec in 1959)
TON 792

1959
Austin Healey 3000
SMO 744 (3rd, 1959 Liège-Rome-Liège)
SMO 745 (4th, 1959 RAC)
SMO 746 (2nd, 1959 German)

1960
SJB 471 (3rd, 1960 RAC)
URX 727 (2nd, 1960 French Alpine, 1st, 1960 Liège-Rome-Liège)

1961
UJB 143
XJB 870
XJB 871 (3rd, 1961 Acropolis)
XJB 872

XJB 876 (1st, 1961 French Alpine)
XJB 877 (2nd, 1961 RAC)

1962
37 ARX (2nd in category, 1963 Tulip)
47 ARX
57 ARX (1st, 1962 French Alpine)
67 ARX (2nd, 1962 RAC)
77 ARX (3rd, 1962 French Alpine, 2nd, 1962 Polish, 3rd, 1962 RAC)

1964
ARX 91B (1st, 1964 Austrian Alpine)
ARX 92B (1st in category, 1964 Tulip, 2nd, 1964 French Alpine)
BMO 93B (1st, 1964 Spa-Sofia-Liège)
BRX 852B (2nd, 1964 RAC)

1965
DRX 257C
DRX 258C (2nd in category, 1965 French Alpine)
EJB 806C (2nd, 1965 RAC)

1967
PWB 57 (re-registered from the earlier ARX 92B)

Index

Note: There are so many mentions of the Austin Healey 100/6 and 3000 rally cars on individual pages, that I have made no attempt to index them.

Revealed by managers
Marcus Chambers
Stuart Turner
Peter Browning

BMC Competitions Department Secrets

By Marcus Chambers, Peter Browning & Stuart Turner

Hardback • 192 pages
£ 24.99* • ISBN: 978-1-904788-68-3

The revealing and surprising inside story of the legendary BMC Works Competitions Department told by the three Competition Managers. This book reveals the inner workings and machinations of one of the most successful motor sport teams Britain has ever seen. Based on previously unpublished internal memos and documents, and the recollections of the prime movers, it describes the ups and downs, and the politics of big time competition in an exciting era. An excellent and entertaining read, and an important factual document, no motor sport enthusiast should be without this book.

" ... some of the best stories, some of the most fascinating facts and some of the most intriguing images we have seen in recent times. And that's no exaggeration." *Classic Car Mart*

"No MG and British motor sport enthusiast should be without this 192 page book." MG Drivers Club

"This is a fun read, detailing the underbelly of BMC's competition department ... The images are wonderful ... Excellent stuff." *Motorsport*

*p&p extra. Prices subject to change.

£14.99* • ISBN 978-1-845840-40-2
This book describes the birth, development, and rallying career of the original Ford Escort, one of Europe's landmark rally cars, in the early 1970s, providing a compact and authoritative history of where, how and why it became so important to the sport.

"Ford Escort MkI is a great read for any old school rally lovers." *Classic Ford*

Ford
Escort Mk1

RALLY GIANTS

Graham Robson

Peugeot
205 T16

RALLY GIANTS

Graham Robson

£14.99* • ISBN 978-1-845841-29-4
This book describes the birth, development, and rallying career of the Peugeot 205 T16, listing each and every success and notable car, tracing exactly how the machinery developed, and improved, from one season to the next.
It provides a compact and authoritative history of where, how and why it became so important to the sport.

*p&p extra. Prices subject to change.

£14.99* • ISBN 978-1-84584-041-9

This book describes the birth, development, and rallying career of the Lancia Stratos, Europe's very first purpose-built rally car, in the mid/late 1970s, providing a compact and authoritative history of where, when and how it became so important to the sport.

"Robson's book is absolutely essential for Lancia and rally enthusiasts, and great for anyone interested in Italian cars in general." VeloceToday.com

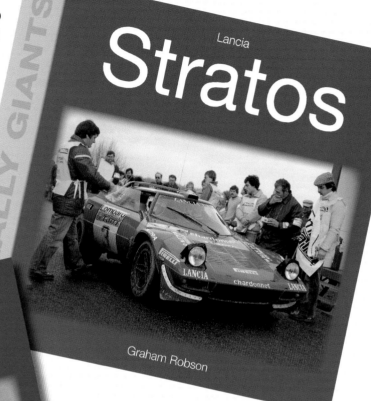

£14.99* • ISBN 978-1-84584-042-6

This book describes the birth, development, and rallying car of the turbocharged, four-wheel-drive Subaru Impreza in the 1990s and early 2000s. It provides a compact and authoritative history of where, how and why it became so important to the sport.

"If you're a rally buff, or just love Subaru's muscled-up monster, this is the perfect book for you to pursue." Hot4s.com.au

*p&p extra. Prices subject to change.

Rallye Sport Fords
By Mike Moreton

£24.99* • ISBN 978-1-845841-15-7
This book charts of the creation of
Rallye Sport Fords in the 70s and 80s.
Popular with enthusiasts, essential for
works teams and affordable enough
for private owners to compete in
motor sport, these performance cars
achieved phenomenal success in
rallying and racing.

This is the story behind the Rallye
Sport cars, from dream to reality,
how and why they happened, the
political arguments, the failures and
successes.

*p&p extra. Prices subject to change.